# Newspaper Shoes

poems

# Penny Perry

Garden Oak Press
Rainbow, California

Garden Oak Press
1953 Huffstatler St., Suite A
Rainbow, CA 92028
760 728-2088
gardenoakpress.com
gardenoakpress@gmail.com

© Penny Perry    All rights reserved

No part of this book may be reproduced, stored in a retrieval system or transmitted by any means without the express written consent of the Publisher.

First published by Garden Oak Press on September 15, 2022

ISBN-13: 978-1-7350556-5-7

Library of Congress Control Number: 2022937588

Printed in the United States of America

The views expressed in this collection of poems are solely those of the poet and do not necessarily reflect the views of the Publisher, and the Publisher hereby disclaims any responsibility for them.

# Contents

### Often I think of the beautiful town
### That is seated by the sea...

| | |
|---|---|
| The Palm Haven Apartments | 4 |
| The Woman with Newspaper Shoes | 6 |
| Ocean Park, California—1950 | 7 |
| A Gold Thimble | 8 |
| The Brownie | 9 |
| Jenny's Latkes | 10 |
| Descendants of Odessa | 12 |
| Meeting the San Joaquin at Union Station | 13 |
| Grandfather Arguing with God | 14 |
| Two White Moths | 16 |
| Soap Bubble Castles | 18 |
| Jane Powell in the Elevator at Bullock's Tea Room | 19 |
| Girls and Boys on the Carlisle Avenue Bus | 20 |
| Shaking Me Awake | 21 |
| Coyotes Eating Apricots | 22 |
| Dear Great Uncles | 23 |
| My Mother and I Pretend We're in Paris | 24 |

### My Mother Still Talks to Me

| | |
|---|---|
| The Nash Metropolitan | 26 |
| Black Velvet | 28 |
| Post Menopausal Robe | 30 |
| Holdfast | 31 |
| The Good Daughter | 32 |
| Letter to My 16-Year-Old Self | 33 |
| Losing My Mother Twice | 34 |
| My Mother Dead Less Than a Year | 35 |
| Not the Daughter Who Was Missed | 36 |
| Woman Inside a Woodstove | 37 |
| My Mother's Letter to Her Best Friend | 38 |
| My Mother Still Talks to Me | 40 |
| Letter from My Mother Who Died at 43 | 41 |

### My Marilyn Hair

| | |
|---|---|
| Girl's Work | 45 |
| My Marilyn Hair | 46 |
| Apartment Hunting with Anita | 47 |
| My Stepmother Kicks Me Out Because I'm Not a Virgin | 48 |
| Home Movies | 49 |
| 501 Valley Drive | 50 |

## Like Mother, Like Daughter

| | |
|---|---|
| Snowing in Tilden Park | 52 |
| Hospital Garden | 53 |
| The Sounds of Your Leaving | 54 |
| The Order of Things | 55 |
| Hanging Up Her Clothes | 56 |
| Putting Out the Fire | 57 |
| Vigil | 58 |
| Patients in Pajamas | 59 |

## What Women Do

| | |
|---|---|
| After Charlottesville | 63 |
| An Iranian Woman Watches the Protest of Neda's Death | 64 |
| Meeting Place | 66 |
| Woman with Shopping Cart Sings to the Sea | 67 |
| The Woman in Space 23 | 68 |
| Jane Austen's Desk | 69 |
| At the Brontë Parsonage | 70 |
| The Mothers of the Mentally Ill | 71 |
| Office Hours, 1979 | 72 |
| Spring, after a Long, Cold Berkeley Winter | 73 |
| Truants from the Suburbs | 74 |
| Moon Dance | 75 |
| I Find Po Chu-I in the Mountains | 76 |
| Reading Po Chu-I on a Rainy Night, I Dance Sometimes | 77 |
| Gladiators' Houses in Ruins by the Roman Coliseum | 78 |
| The New Drug | 79 |
| Virginia's Boots | 80 |
| Lentil Soup | 81 |
| What Women Do | 82 |
| Her Breasts Still Full of Milk | 83 |

## Mothers and Sons

| | |
|---|---|
| The News | 86 |
| How You Began | 87 |
| Proposal | 88 |
| The Guides | 89 |
| The House on Dover Street | 90 |
| Plenty | 91 |
| Loving Tiffany | 92 |
| The Lake of Swans | 94 |
| On the Anniversary | 96 |
| Wigwam | 97 |
| Seen from the Hayes Street Bus | 98 |
| My Son Calls on My Birthday to Say He Bought His First House | 99 |

| | |
|---|---|
| On the Eve of Your 39th Birthday | 100 |
| House in Summer | 101 |
| We Sit Up Half the Night | 102 |
| For My Son on His Divorce | 103 |

## Family

| | |
|---|---|
| Famous Flexible Straws | 106 |
| Carlos Called to Tell My Mother Her Husband Was a Cheating Dog | 107 |
| Breakfast at Starbucks | 108 |
| Reading Sexton's *The Black Art* on our Anniversary | 109 |
| Gardenias | 110 |
| After an Argument | 112 |
| Pillows | 113 |
| The Nights I Called | 114 |
| The Tree of White Peaches | 115 |
| Visitors | 116 |
| My Daughter's Breath | 117 |
| Here at the Border of Some Country I Don't Know | 118 |
| Four Weeks after Her Stroke | 119 |
| Portland Report | 120 |
| Fig Bars | 122 |
| Reading Poetry in Portland | 123 |

## Lessons from the Chaparral

| | |
|---|---|
| Father Seahorse | 126 |
| Eve's Task | 127 |
| Lessons from the Chaparral | 128 |
| Pact | 129 |
| Buying Rain Barrels in a Drought | 130 |

## Absent Friends

| | |
|---|---|
| Her Mail Unopened on the Table | 132 |
| After His TV Dinner | 133 |
| Requiem for Johnny | 134 |
| Minnow from Steve | 135 |
| I'm in the Same White Shirt | 136 |

## Each Morning I Sip Green Tea

| | |
|---|---|
| The Appointment | 138 |
| 5 a.m. | 139 |
| Bats at Twilight | 140 |
| Po Chu-I, Me, and a Thousand Fears | 141 |
| Two Venuses | 142 |
| My Mother the Pantheist | 143 |
| Each Week My Husband Buys Our Groceries | 144 |
| Each Morning I Sip Green Tea | 145 |

| | |
|---|---|
| Acknowledgments | 146 |
| Credits | 146 |
| Gratitude | 147 |
| About the Poet | 148 |

# Also by Penny Perry

### *poetry*

## Santa Monica Disposal & Salvage
[Garden Oak Press: 2012]

### *fiction*

## Selling Pencils, and Charlie
[Lymer & Hart: 2020]
Finalist, San Diego Book Awards (2020)

# Praise for Penny Perry

**from Marge Piercy:**

"SANTA MONICA DISPOSAL & SALVAGE is a powerful and moving collection of poems that form a narrative of loss and survival. Perry's attitude is incredibly nonjudgmental in these poems, rich in detail, grounded in a place and time. They are dense with specifics but flow in carefully crafted, effortless-seeming narrative."

**from Diane Wakoski:**

"I loved everything about SANTA MONICA DISPOSAL & SALVAGE. The vivid details of place, period, people, the rich linking narrative, and most of all the sense of poetry being teased out of the everyday world imposed on the immigrant experience of her grandparents, the echoes of the holocaust, the odd snazzy world of movie dominated California before digitized reality usurped it. . .I who recognize personality in art was completely won over by these poems."

**from Maria Mazziotti Gillan:**

"SANTA MONICA DISPOSAL & SALVAGE is sad and funny at the same time. . .rooted in memory and place and laced with a sardonic, self-deprecating humor. Best of all, it refuses to give up, to give in even in the face of tragedy and humiliation. . .It is a hymn to the life force that is so evident in this narrator, her forgiveness, her vulnerability, her effervescence.

**from Laura Boss:**

In SELLING PENCILS, AND CHARLIE, Penny Perry effortlessly creates a remarkable coming-of-age novel through the first person voice of a young female protagonist reminiscent of a female Holden Caulfield. . . (She) deserves a following as vast as Judy Blume in her adult novels.

**from Kirkus Reviews:**

An engaging novel, featuring a winning character who. . . seems to learn little from the cautionary tales of Jane Austen and the Brontës. . .until (she) abandons her dependence on unreliable men and makes hard choices. . .As a result, SELLING PENCILS, AND CHARLIE is a beguiling volume.

for Bill

# The Woman with Newspaper Shoes

poems

## Penny Perry

Often I think of
 the beautiful town
That is seated
 by the sea. . .

*My Lost Youth*
— Henry Wadsworth Longfellow

# The Palm Haven Apartments

Mrs. Frances X. Bushman, abandoned
by her silent-screen star husband
for his leading lady, shares our square patio.
Our two apartments sit above the garage.
She complains to the landlord, Mr. Palmquist,
about our yipping Cairn Terrier, and me stomping
in my father's shoes early Sunday morning
while she's putting on her hat for Mass.

All night awake and in my dreams
I hear the squeal of garage doors opening,
the hush of engines, the good night slam
of the closing car doors. My dad used to
work the late shift at Douglas Aircraft.
Now he's laid off and does odd jobs.

Plump in my plaid dress, and chewing my braids,
I trail after my parents on our Sunday afternoon walks.
My mother wears her Katharine Hepburn slacks. We're not
supposed to walk on the apartment's grassy front lawn
or touch the two palm trees imported from the Riviera
or the sign that reads *Palm Haven Apartments*.

We turn right on San Vicente Boulevard.
I take three steps on Anna May Wong's stone ledge
and jump off. If the famous actress ever opened her curtains,
she could see me and be mad.

We stop at the park with the Totem pole.
Mother looks at the cliffs, the Pacific Ocean and pier.
She sighs at the sight of Marion Davies' mansion
on the sand. "So many movie stars," she says.
"The beach looks just like the postcard."
"Ritzy," my father says.

Mrs. Bushman tells me if I'm quiet Sunday
mornings, we can listen to Jack Benny on her radio
at 3. We both laugh when a stickup man asks,
"Your money or your life"—and Jack hesitates:
"I'm thinking, I'm thinking!" he says.

Right at Sunday twilights, my parents drop me off
at my grandmother's. They tell me to keep
it a secret that they hurry back to the park, beach
and pier to collect glass bottles of Coca-Cola
and other sodas. They scan the sand for pennies,
nickels, dimes and quarters. Sometimes
they even find paper dollars to help pay the rent
at the Palm Haven Apartments.

# The Woman with Newspaper Shoes

Faded babushka on her head. Her face
wide as Grandpa's. She must be
from Russia too. She weaves around tar
on the sand, and pelicans that Grandpa
says are dead from DDT. She's wrapped
newspaper around her feet, tied the paper
with twine. Yesterday's Sunday colored
funnies on her left foot. I can see Nancy's
black hair, and Blondie's yellow.
Grandpa's polished leather shoes glint
in the mist. My new sandals have straps.
The woman's paper shoes rattle
in the sea breeze. I can't stop staring.
 "Grandpa, why?" I ask. His answer dies
in the croak of the fog horn.

# Ocean Park, California — 1950

*for my grandfather*

The old men in yarmulkes sit
at card tables—flimsy, unstable
in the wind.

After the wars, after the pogroms—
pinochle and borscht at noon,
ocean and fog. the smell
of fish from the market,
synagogue steps the color of salt.

Across town the bells of Saint Monica's
chime the hour.

The old men remember village bells
at Easter, how those bells sang:
"Christ killers. Christ killers."
How soon after Church bells
the Cossacks came.

The old men in yarmulkes still hear
the horses hooves,
the hiss of houses on fire.

Salt from the ocean on their lips,
the old men in America,
stare at the sea,

hear the prayers of waves.

# A Gold Thimble

*for my grandmother*

Her brothers and sisters-in-law bought
the thimble for her golden anniversary.
She said she earned the gift for 50 years
of feeding her husband's clan roast chicken,
gefilte fish, chopped liver.
She called one of the sisters (Frances)
*High, Wide, and Handsome* for her big behind.
She named the other (Mae) *Broom Face.*
(She loved Frances, hated Mae.)
Too small, the thimble perched
on her plump finger like a too-small nest.
That same thimble swallowed my thumb
like a fairy skirt. My grandmother sang
along with Caruso, stitched my plaid skirts
and wool jumpers on her Singer sewing machine.
I'd never be a seamstress. My lazy left eye
and my good right eye each saw a separate needle,
a separate row of stitches. I loved the thimble's border
of red rubies. *A bloody noose,* she'd say.
The skirt or jumper finished, she'd take the thimble,
warm from my hand, set it like a hump of gold ice
on a shelf next to an empty bone china cup.
*Some day this will be yours.*

# The Brownie

You stare at the camera. Your friend Leslie grins.
She is practically saluting.
It will take you 30 years to whisper:
"My father was a drunk."
She will tell you, "Oh everyone knew."

Your ex-friend-turned-nemesis, Patti,
is plumper, smaller, and meaner
than you remembered. Tall, skinny,
tow-headed Kathy, future editor
of *Sunset Magazine*, fights a smirk.

The girls of Troop 55 look respectable,
all except you. Your illegal sweater has slipped off
your shoulder. Your beanie sits like
an upside-down dog dish on your head.

Wet ribbon and chewed hair escape your braid.
Your torn uniform hem points at pudgy legs.
Silent clown Brownie from long ago, I want
to brush your hair, wipe that smudge from your face.

Just when I'm ready to give up on you, I see
an alertness in those wide eyes. Maybe
the twisted belt and untied shoes are code,
a shout that says, "Not happy when hiking,"
when you mean, "Even Brownie Troop 55 can't stop
chairs from flying across my living room."

Maybe you're telling the camera, stout Troop leader
Mrs. Lawson, even me—the grown up you:
"I have my secrets."

# Jenny's Latkes

Just the sweet smell of onions
and potatoes browning in hot oil
led me down dark stairs
from my grandparents house
to the basement apartment
my great aunts called home.

Jenny stood at the stove.
Wisps of gray streaked
her strawberry-blond hair.
An apron curved over her belly,
a belly that once that had housed
her only child, the one
she was forced to give away.

Jenny mangled two languages:
Yiddish and English. Like me,
she was "a little slow."
Her latkes were a work of art.

Over the sizzle of oil,
and Aunt Bella's sing-song
of market prices—"Bumble Bee
salmon, 49 cents"—Aunt Jenny
smiled her secret smile
and waited for the moment
before the oil spattered
to nudge her cakes with a spatula.

One quick flip, the sizzle,
now a hum, then on to a plate.
She presented her golden
brown cakes to me.

The lightness, oh the lightness
of those satisfying cakes.

Grandma knocked on the door
one holiday morning. She seldom
interrupted my visits with her sisters.
She said Bella would report everything,
word-for-word, later. That morning,
she told us, Jenny had a visitor.

A young man, with polished shoes,
gray flannel slacks and jacket,
and strawberry-blond hair,
stepped down the stairs.

He stared at me, then Aunt Bella,
then the woman who stood at the stove,
spatula in hand. He smiled:
"It took so long for me to find you."

# Descendants of Odessa

*for Isaac Babel*

    *after his short story, Awakening*

Isaac, hero to all those
inept Jewish descendants of Odessa,
who may be born in families of musicians,
but can't hold a bow to a violin,
or tease melodies from piano keys.
Our grandparents in soft black cloth
chant and pray for us. Luckier
than you, they escaped the Cossacks,
became cantors, shopkeepers,
shoemakers, and tailors in America.
Descendants of the *shtetl*,
summer freckles—puny brown polka dots—
speckle our broad Russian faces.
We learn the names of trees:
birch, acacia, palm.
Allergic to native grasses,
we cough and sneeze.
Our skins blossom with hives.
On pudgy, unsteady feet, we traipse
through thorny bushes. Our sea,
like yours, sparkles before us.
Our Odessa grandmothers
smear thick Noxzema
on our arms, legs, and faces.
Rubber bathing caps pinch,
and redden our ears.
At last, thinking of you,
we plunge into the water.
Waves crack against our knees.
We rise like Sabbath dough.
The sea tastes like Passover salt.
You were right, Isaac:
the sea does hold us.

# Meeting the San Joaquin at Union Station

*for Wendy*

As if already in cahoots with you, I woke at dawn,
400 miles away in the inland valley town where
you boarded the *San Joaquin*. For me, the clock didn't move,
summer never started until after you arrived. At last,
they were ready. Grandpa, in a suit and hat, mamboing
with the gas pedal. Grandma, with her picnic basket
firm on her lap (because they might forget to feed you
on the train). And me, in pedal pushers and a pony tail,
to prove that unlike you, I would never grow up.
I would be a tomboy forever. In winter, away from you,
I wore skirts, and even braided ribbons in my hair.
We were always hours early, but it was better
there at Union Station, with your train listed
on the schedule board, as if it really was going to arrive.

Always shorter, always younger, I waited
for the next installment of life in your sinful valley town.
Parents took off their clothes. Boys drove fancy Chevys with fins.
You would tell me the shocking books you read: *Peyton Place*, *Lady
Chatterley's Lover*, and the latest family secret (the boy
who shot himself because he loved my mother),
and the strange hair growing on you down there. Later
we would fight—real live hair-pulling fights—as if
we really were sisters, not just cousins.

All this coming to me roaring through the Central Valley
behind the single, bright light of the *San Joaquin*.

On the platform, grandma whispered:
"The little one didn't wash her face."
The *San Joaquin Daylight* wheezed to a stop.
After our first fight, I'd be wheezing too, but when
the doors banged open, that was always far away.
Like Grace Kelly in white, you stepped lightly off the train.
Over Grandpa's shy embrace, you whispered
the first secret of our summer.

# Grandfather Arguing with God

Sitting in your purple wing chair
reading Bertrand Russell
or arguing with Aquinas
about God,

no wizened Grandpa
with a corncob pipe,
you were a savvy whale
of a man.

No vices, except lust
for your wife's roast chicken,
her matzo ball soup,

and your need to give
your granddaughters, both
future poets, daily tests
from the *Readers Digest*
"Thirty Days to a More
Powerful Vocabulary."

We hated your rules:
be on time, maintain
the cleanest of clothes,
scholarship is discipline.

You, once the boy
in the *shtetl*,
hiding from Cossacks
in a chicken coop,

learning to read and write
in Hebrew, would at 70
smell of fresh shoe polish
and sweet cologne.

You swam in the Pacific
every day, even in winter.
We'd stand on the shore,
seaweed wrapped around our ankles,
tar in our toes,

and watch you shoulder
through the waves.
Some misty mornings
you were the only swimmer,

the one whale without its mate,
raising a fin
to the god you never believed
was there.

We were teenagers when you died:
one furious you disapproved
of her Catholic boyfriend,
the other banned by you
for her flirtation
with a distant cousin.

Only now, both of us
the age you were then,
can say you gave us
your vocabulary,
your insistence on the right detail.

Before poetry readings,
we polish our shoes.
We admit we're granddaughters
of the *shtetl*, we learned to read,
to write, to shoulder through
cold waves of the Pacific.
Even on unfriendly mornings,
we shine for you.

# Two White Moths

*after Cecilia Wolloch*

*for my cousin, Wendy*

I'm sitting in our past
in the little add-on room.
Grandpa and his friends
up the three short stairs
in the kitchen, drinking
tea, playing pinochle.

Two girls in light cotton,
reprimanded for some
small wrong. I crayoned
your Kodak face purple.
You pinched my pale,
plump skin.
We are on our backs,
counting knots
in the pine ceiling.
Eugenia berries heavy
at the window.

Our own white-haired-
Old-Testament-God
Grandpa pronounced us
evil, and we believed.
In his sonorous voice
he told us above the knotty
pine, there is only sky,
some arresting
constellations, Orion,
the Pleiades.
No heaven for your
mother, already lost,
he said, or mine
soon to fly away.

You tug my hair, I kick
your knee. Two white
moths fly in the window.
The whir of their wings
a mother's lullaby.
The moths find our lamp.
Bodies soft as Q-tips,
one alights in your hair,
the second settles
on the down of my arm.

# Soap Bubble Castles

*for my cousin Wendy*

With her swirl of skirts and suds,
our socialist grandmother's soap-bubble castles
got razed into huts by her strong fingers.

No washer or dryer in the beach town
bungalow where you and I grew up.
Our grandmother scrubbed clothes
in the long oval of her bathtub.

Wet sheets and blankets filled
the laundry basket. Too heavy a load
for her to lug to the line strung across
the back of the narrow yard.

Eugenia bushes with purple berries
supported a bloom of Grandpa's
Brooks Brothers' shirts, Grandma's
nightgowns, corsets, and large harness bras.

My grandfather, the retired lawyer,
called from his wing chair:
*Use the clothesline! Don't be a peasant!*

From branches of the Eugenia bushes,
our red pedal pushers waved
like revolutionary flags.

This morning, the second of your visit,
muttering about the neighbors,
my husband sends me out to remove
our sexy underwear from the bushes.

A ruby-throated hummingbird sings
above your panties on the flowering yellow
hibiscus. My negligee lifts its lacy folds
above a purple spear of lavender.

# Jane Powell in the Elevator at Bullock's Tea Room

Her face steamy, a kettle on the boil,
my mother says: *If you keep eating
the only job you'll get is fat lady in the circus.*
She hands me a note:
>*Prunes, eleven calories
>unbuttered toast, one hundred.
>Picture a pound of potatoes and
>imagine them on your inner thighs.*

My thighs do look like mashed potatoes.
She frowns at movie magazines
spread open on the kitchen table.
*You have your father's frame.
You'll never be as thin as Jane Powell.
Or Debbie Reynolds. Bite for bite,
I'll diet with you.*
I cover my flesh with a red, woolen coat,
and, like Sydney Greenstreet in a noir movie,
travel back alleys, peer over trash cans
spy on my friends in bathing suits
sauntering to the beach.
A fat girl can be a poet. I thumb-tack
Amy Lowell, with her whiskers
and voluminous skirt, on my bedroom wall.
I leave enough food on my plate to feed villages
of bloated children. I dream of cheese,
of mayo. To celebrate my success,
my mother takes me to a fashion show.
Jane Powell in a linen suit steps into the elevator.
Her cornflower blue eyes are even more stunning
than in the movies. She looks away
from our tape-measure stares. As if longing
to pin herself paper doll style, hip to hip,
my mother inches closer to Jane.

My mother's breasts have shrunk, her hips
are horseshoes. She is a swizzle stick,
a scarecrow in need of stuffing. Under my coat
I feel my own twig arms. The elevator dings.
Jane glides to the tearoom, where women taller and thinner
than the famous actress model fall fashions.

# Girls and Boys on the Carlisle Avenue Bus

Tall girls slumped. Shy girls hid
behind glasses, books, bulky
sweaters. Melissa, with pierced
ears, wearing a tight red dress,
looked like an apple ready for picking.
Our breasts in training bras,
or cups, A, B, C, and even D
jiggled every time the Carlisle Avenue
bus hit a pot hole. In our plaid skirts,
stockings, flats, the bus carried us away
from our swing set, orange tree backyards.
Boys, jostled, nudged each other.
They smelled like citrus Jell-O
salad mold, their dads' aftershave.
Out the window, lifting fog
revealed the seedy part of town.
Pete's Pawn Shop, palm trees
with browning jowls, a neon
silhouette of a cocktail waitress.
Bad boy Johnny Angelo, a swirl
of gelled black hair,
full kissable lips, a bee
thirsty for pollen, leaned close.
Our nubby blue notebooks
slipping from our hands,
*amo, amas, amat,*
the only Latin verb we could remember.

## Shaking Me Awake

The neighbor, Maxie, raises his glass of ginger ale:
"Next year Jerusalem." Grandpa purses thick lips:
"Folly. A Jewish ghetto in the desert."

My grandmother sighs. Roast chicken cold on the platter.
Matzo ball soup barely touched. Every New Year's Eve,
the same fight.

I wriggle in my chair. A week ago, two smiling Israelis—
Sabras, they called themselves—in work shirts and jeans
dug up the fully-grown lemon tree in my mother's backyard.

They said my tree would grow next to bananas and mangos.
They wrapped the tree's roots and California soil in a burlap bag.
I pictured myself sturdy in shorts, living in a kibbutz,

feeding goats, hoeing soil. Sabra sounded so romantic, lush fruit
of the prickly pear cactus, idiomatic for an Israeli-born Jew.
Never mind I was allergic to desert air.

"Maxie, you have a house, a business, a garden."
Grandpa leans back in his chair, arms strong from his daily swim
almost hide his paunch. "Assimilate and you're safe."

"Safe?" Maxie rubs his balding head. "German Jews were
assimilated." Grandpa winces at Maxie's accent,
secretly calls him, "The Little Yiddle."

"My cousins butchered in Auschwitz. And you?"
Maxie turns to Grandpa. "The pogroms. No picnic."
Every New Year's Eve Grandpa tells us about Cossacks

on horsebacks. Soldiers with fur hats, red uniforms, burning
houses, killing Jews. Tonight he says, "Now we're soldiers,
killers, destroying homes, olive groves."

The mantle clock chimes the hour. I fall asleep
in the add-on room, in percale sheets bought just for me:
*Those two Sabras, one driving a tractor, the other a bulldozer, aren't smiling.*

*Even in moonlight I can see furrows in their foreheads.*
*Big wheels rumble closer. Gray limbs and branches*
*of my lemon tree in the tractor's teeth.*

Grandpa, his big hands on my shoulder, shakes me awake.

# Coyotes Eating Apricots

*for my cousin, Wendy*

This morning, a coyote,
lean as bamboo, eats apricots
fallen from our tree.
Our cat, safe from him at last,
sleeps under the porch.
My fists uncurl. Curses turn
to honey on my lips.
No longer a wild predator,
this coyote is a stray dog,
already too thin at summer's end.

I think of our feral childhood,
the way you, a little girl, vamped men,
the flesh-eating lies you told.
Our house rocked
with your tsunami tantrums.
You were a lion-sized chameleon,
roaring the shutters down,
while I kept so quiet,
even I forgot I was there.

Now, I pretend
Grandma sits you in a high chair,
calls you "child," wraps a lacy bib
around your neck, sings you lullabies,
and serves you those stewed apricots
you craved.

## Dear Great Uncles

You were like Grandpa's metal-folding chairs
set out every summer under the gazebo,
part of hot July's scenery, like zinnias
and Grandma's ruby borscht. Uncle Al
with his fat, smelly cigars and Dodger cap.
Max so beautiful, a model, a Greek God
with turquoise eyes. Dick, a human kickball,
even happy with American potato salad,
and hen-pecked by his wife.

Grandpa's brothers, escapees
from the Russian pogroms, safe now
with their glasses of hot tea, pinochle, and politics.
McCarthy's voice on the radio is worrisome, but
not as terrifying as the ground-shaking hooves
announcing Cossacks. Grandpa's brothers, sweat
under the armpits of crisp shirts concealing big bellies
(except for Max), sit open-mouthed like baby vultures
desperate for Grandma's chicken soup.

A girl in braids, I wanted to be like all of you,
wave my arms, shout my thoughts on every topic. No one
told me the set director would take each of you away,
one by one, like summer chairs, rickety metal skeletons,
their striped fabric faded and unraveled, leaving
banners of loose thread.

# My Mother and I Pretend We're in Paris

in an outside café with red geraniums
on the white wrought iron table,
and not in our kitchen, its worn teapot,
Woolworth's lamp,
where we wait for my father
who is late again.
We don't admit we're hungry,

the pot roast with sweet carrots
simmering on the stove,
or wonder if he is drunk
with another woman.
We dine "Continental." Caesar
salad first, forking poor little anchovies,
and home-made croutons. We split

an English muffin, now pretending
we're in a tea shop on the High Street
of an English village.
Beef and carrot-scented steam rising
from the stove, our stomachs
complaining, our shirts stuck
to the backs of our old chairs,

we read our favorite E. F. Benson's village tale:
how Miss Mapp sneaked into
the kitchen of her rival, Lucia,
to find the secret ingredient
in the lobster recipe
that lying Lucia hid from her friends.

# My Mother Still Talks to Me

# The Nash Metropolitan

*for my mother*

Driving to the grocery store
I see an old Nash Metropolitan for sale
at the side of the road.
Saddle shoe black and white,
squat, wide-faced, its grille grins.

You dreamed of a Metropolitan for me.
Egg yolk yellow and white,
a magic coach to fly me to the university.
Still, with a cruel push of your broom, you'd brood:
"You don't work hard enough.
You're such a California girl."

You hated palm trees, birds of paradise,
the slow drawls of transplanted Iowans.
In high heels, you clicked past neighbors in their shorts.
You had two Master's Degrees and no outside job.
Peering over my Latin, I'd think,
I'll never be stuck like you.

Now, you swoop down from a saddle shoe black sky.
You swat dust on my table.
"If you must do domestic work, do it well."

I tell you, "You missed the women's movement."
Your chin is stubborn: "Susan B. Anthony."

"The second women's movement. Betty Freidan.
The pill. Panty hose." I lift my skirt
"No more belts or snaps."

In moonlight, your 43-year-old face
looks so young to me now.

You peer at black print, my words on my white screen.
"What is this?" you ask.
"Poetry. My vehicle. The way I like to travel."
You read, sigh. "Not bad."
Grateful you didn't sweep my words away,
I offer you the gift I've waited years to give:
"You weren't alone.
All over America women wanted more."
You nod, drifting past the bird of paradise.

Grocery day, I see the Metropolitan,
its impudent face pointing toward the road.
All these years we have been the martyred woman,
the accusing girl.
Maybe you would have left my father.
We could have driven my Metropolitan
up the coast together, the Pacific whizzing by,
your husky *instruction* voice purring.
"If you can drive, you can go anywhere.
Press the clutch. Give it gas, gas, gas."

# Black Velvet

*for my mother*

In the dressing room I take a deep
breath  make my belly flat,
think of you in your velvet suit
Grandma copied from *Vogue*

that last winter.
Stitching on her old Singer
she had grumbled:
"That crazy dieting will kill

my daughter."
Ten pounds heavier than you
ever were. I turn in the full
length mirror,

"Picture apples around your waist,
even spilling out of your shoes,"
you once said.

You drank vinegar, dropped cigarette
ashes on tea room sandwiches,
then binged on pickled herring brine.
Dieting killed you.

I buried your beauty magazines
in our back yard and grew
into one of those dowdy women
you despised, a dumpling in pedal
pushers, no make-up, hiding

in loose shirts. Nights, I asked
did you want to die or did you
believe a thinner you
would reel your husband home?

I exhale, wriggle tug into size 10
black slacks, run my hand along
the velvet nap. "Velvet's so elegant,"
you said on our trip to New York.

Under a hotel awning, you stood
smiling at the Manhattan sidewalk.
Your white satin blouse gleamed
like the falling snow.

I breathe, button the slacks,
and rummage through the torn
lining of my purse, for the tube
of lipstick I buried there.

# Post Menopausal Robe

*for my mother*

On mornings when you were out
buying groceries, I shrugged off my chenille robe
and slipped into your peignoir. Puffy sleeves, pearl
buttons, the white organdy robe had a pink rose
pinned at the "bosom,"
a girl's Sweet 16 or communion dress.
My father blamed your hysterectomy for his affair.
"She didn't want me," he said over his beer.
I thought this was another of his lies, then read
two years after menopause begins, desire comes back.

I saw you at the Sample Shop, palming nickels
and quarters from your household allowance,
lifting the robe from the rack.
How pretty you looked in your new robe,
prowling our house after midnight, fresh lipstick,
waiting for him.
After you died, your robe gave me nightmares.
You died fast, a heart attack at 43.
In my dreams, it took you months to die.
Lying in bed, your face pale against the pillow,

you'd ask me to bring you your robe. I'd roll open
the wardrobe door. Instead of the white organdy,
my father's lover's red slip hung in your closet.
I'd try to block your view of those red tiers.
I'd slam the door but you always saw the whirling
Flamenco dancer skirt. The afternoon I packed
your clothes away, I rolled open the wardrobe
door, took out your robe and held it next to me.
The puffy sleeves looked limp. A safety pin
gleamed behind the flattened rose.

# Holdfast

*for my mother*

I should have ignored the nurse's
warning and tiptoed across the hall.
Overnight, your bedroom had become
a tunnel to the unknown. The oxygen
tent humming and puffing, you so small
under that pulsating jelly fish.

I should have laced our fingers together
like strands of kelp in a ball at the beach.
I should have held you back from the tide.

# The Good Daughter

*after Joe Weil*

After her heart attack, my mother,
small in the nightgown
she had accidentally dyed
vomit green, whispered:

*I have to live for you.*
Just yesterday, an ordinary Tuesday,
I heard her tell her friend Dorothy
I was a rewarding girl.

The home care nurse, nicknamed Miss Bedpan
by my mother, marched into the room
with Saltine Crackers that would somehow
save her patient. My mother,

nestled on my father's side of the bed,
asked, *Does he care?*
I hadn't seen him for hours.
I said of course he cares,

of course she'd be fine. Not lies.
I was 16. Nothing bad had happened.
The nurse shooed me out.
Not hungry for the bologna sandwich

my mother had made for my school
lunch, foreign prayers on my lips,
I paced the quiet house. I sneaked
in once. The nurse dozing, magazine

on her lap. My mother under
an oxygen tent.
I lay on my bed, drumbeat of the song,
*Running Bear* on my Motorola radio.

Thinking of a boy I met New Year's Eve,
crew cut, woolly brown bear sweater,
I slid my fingers under my panties.
My mother's heart failing,

a stranger to myself,
my nipples hard,
no longer a good daughter,
my own heart beat faster.

# Letter to My 16-Year-Old Self

You tell the Helms Bakery driver
your mother died. Her account closed.

You watch the blue and yellow truck
trundle down the street,
stealing the last of the sweet smell
of bread and cake.

Your own life has crumbled like the palm-
sized cardboard truck, from a long ago
bakery field trip.

I want to tell you more sweets will come.
Even now Suzie, who you stopped talking to,
her wheat-colored cardigan flapping,
is running up the street to comfort you.

I want to tell you, how years from now
your grown daughter will buy you
a *concha* at a Mexican market.
Pink coconut will fill your mouth,

and you'll remember those Saturdays
you and your mother stepped timidly
into the bakery truck.

The truck driver—our Helmsman—opened the dessert drawer,
showed off glazed and sprinkled donuts.
Some Saturdays you and your mother
chose cream puffs. White cream oozed
from puffs of every day popover dough.

# Losing My Mother Twice

After the funeral,
I peer through peepholes
in the oak door that leads
to the living room.

Clink of glasses. Ginger ale.
Manischewitz. My parents' friend Arthur
wears a white shirt and sports jacket.
His wet eyes blink behind glasses.

His wife, Louise, six feet
of golden valkyrie, feeds her husband
gefilte fish on a Ritz. I look for my dad.
He must have slipped away.

My mother told me her romance
with my father was a rich college girl,
hotel bell boy, Washington Square
in the snow, first love story.

My grandfather, his back to me
at the kitchen table, tells a chum,
"She should have stayed married
to Arthur."

*Arthur?* Patent leather pumps
squeeze my toes. Linoleum buckles
under my feet. My mother
said she had no secrets.

Two years ago, the newlyweds
rang the doorbell.
Before my mother turned the knob,
her dark hair piled in a bun,

she asked me: *Do these heels
make me look taller?*

# My Mother Dead Less Than a Year

my father moved in with a hairdresser
and her daughter in an apartment
across town. Scrubbed like a baked
potato ready for the oven,
he'd come to his in-laws
to pay for my room and board.
The smell of dill, the steam
from my grandmother's chicken soup
made his eyes water. He'd stare
at the newly-washed linoleum,

back slowly toward the door
that slammed behind him.
I'd pretend I was asleep
in my bedroom downstairs.
My grandparents would whisper
about him in Yiddish,
"Shicker." And louder about me:
"She forgot to lock the door again."
"She left a mascara stain on my
clean white towel."

# Not the Daughter Who Was Missed

*after Louise Gluck*

She was not the daughter who wrote Broadway plays
so riveting that even Aunt Belle stopped whispering.

She was not the daughter who pinned violets
on a wool suit on a cold spring day.

She was the daughter who drove her famous big sister
to that doctor—the butcher, the abortionist.

She was the daughter who paced nights past framed
photos in her Lady Macbeth gown,

and days drank black tea, scrubbed, bleached spots
on old linoleum that wouldn't come out.

She was not the daughter who was missed until she was.
The mother remembered her daughter who smelled

of Dutch Girl cleanser, the daughter who was once a girl
with a bow. The daughter who once cuddled in her lap.

# Woman Inside a Woodstove

*for my mother*

inside a steel box
hissing
your small door
a square of black iron

woman in a garden hose
spitting
inside all those coils and curls
your coupling
a circle of gold

women were in boxes then
women were in circles

you wanted me warm     you wanted me well
busy burning     busy drowning
you hissed instructions     held up mirrors
waved your maps     opened your small door

I crawled through

# My Mother's Letter to Her Best Friend
*June 5, 1942*

Dear Isabel,

I drove my sister to the doctor's
in Los Angeles. It all happened
so quickly. I promised to bring her
a chocolate phosphate when
it was over.

She joked with the nurses.
Told them if she puked
from ether she would buy
each of them a pair of nylon
stockings.

She insisted on ether because
her friend Hannah had told her
an abortion would be too
painful without it.

In the waiting room, I picked
up a movie magazine.
During the next 10 minutes
I heard a harsh breathing,
as though she were gasping.
I told myself she would breathe
differently under ether.

A nurse rushed to the telephone
to call emergency.
My knees collapsed.
I remember the sounds of sirens
on the street, footsteps on the stairs,
the hissing, horrible sounds
of the oxygen tent.

I remember words like
"her pulse rate is low."
"She has a seven-month-old baby
at home." "Isn't it a pity?"

Finally, the doctor came in
and said, "Your sister is dead."
The bastard didn't even have
the sense to shut the door.
I could see her head thrown back
on the table.
He told me to stop screaming.

# My Mother Still Talks to Me

Not the stories of her childhood,
how she and Isabel skipped school
and bought pastrami sandwiches
and pickles before sneaking
into a new Marx Brothers movie,
or how they failed their interview
at Fieldstone by proclaiming they
loved banned D. H. Lawrence
the best, or how they'd ditch poor
little Rosie Smear by darting into
Macy's and dashing out the back.
Poor Rosie never caught on.

I was sure my mother's childhood
was more interesting than mine.
She died when I was 16.

Now she appears in my kitchen.
I mop grungy linoleum. She wears
a summer dress and heels. The scent
of Shalimar floats over the stove.
She glances at the floor, the grease
on the stove. She says, "Instead
of stories, I should have taught
you how to clean."

In jeans, tee, red bandana,
she sprayed white vinegar
on windows, wrung Dad's
thick work shirts
and hung them on the line.

Now she tells me, "Pour milk
over the sink so you won't
have to clean up a spill.
Save coffee grounds for roses
and blueberries.
Remember to place tulip bulbs
in a brown paper bag in the fridge.
They need winter chill
to bloom in spring."

# Letter from My Mother Who Died at 43

Daughter, my dying, leaving
when you were only 16,
turned you wild.
(Yes, in new jeans we once
planted a perfect English garden
behind a picket fence.)
Dirt in your fingernails,

ragged straw hat, waist deep
in cattails, you coax orchids
from desert soil. When the hawk,
guarding its young, swooped
down knocking the hat from
your un-brushed hair,
digging its talons

into curls I once combed with
my fingers, I would have ducked
as you first did. But would I have then—
startled, and still shaking—straightened
myself and saluted the Red-tail
streaking to the safety of the wire?

# My Marilyn Hair

# Girl's Work

My black-lipped daughter
wants to pierce holes
in her ears and belly.
"Don't mutilate yourself
for boys," I hiss,
as if garter hooks never bruised
twin circles in my thighs, or
my girdle—that angry waffle iron—
never pressed pink diamonds
in my skin, or

I never cried
to my soon-to-be-stepmother,
"My scalp is burning."
My hair wound tightly in rollers,
I tried to escape the dryer,
but Anita, tilting on spike heels
like a lovely palm about to topple,
just laughed.
She was happy in those days.
My wild father had agreed
at last to marry.
"It's girls' work to be beautiful."
She handed me ice water
and pushed me back
into the helmet of fire.

# My Marilyn Hair

Big Anita strips color from my honey hair.
The lips my father loves, so close to my neck.
Ava Gardner glamorous: black hair, low-cut blouse,
drop earrings that sway like pots of gold.
The smell of peroxide fills the tiny apartment.
She says, "This will look so good with your white skin."
Little Anita, 14, her brown face wistful, sings along
with the Beach Boys about surfer girls.
The two Anitas parachuted into my life three days
after my mother died. Big Anita called after midnight:
"Come get your dad. He's scaring me."
Watching my dad and Big Anita's courtship, his stalking,

her *No-No-No—Yes-Yes-Yes*, and their marriage
a year later, I developed a tic in my left eye, covered
my curves with a big shirt. Even in the 100-year-
old novels I read, love made people crazy.
Big Anita runs long fingernails through my scalp.
My hair is purple. I slump under the towel.
I have the lead in *Bus Stop*. Cherie isn't supposed
to have clown hair. Twisting my hair, in rollers,
Big Anita sings about Spanish eyes.
*Spanish Eyes. Surfer Girl.* My neck feels tight.
No one writes songs about girls who button blouses
to their chins.

Little Anita's blond, blue-eyed boyfriend, Surfer Jim,
is at the door. He checks to see if my father is lurking,
then grins. Little Anita is beautiful in the bikini I bought her.
Last week she had cried, "Whoever heard of a Mexican
surfer girl?" Now she will walk with Jim like the girl
from Ipanema, past all those snooty blond Gidgets.
Big Anita tugs at my rollers. I stare at my Marilyn hair,
the pasta-colored spit curl. If my mother were here
she would quote: "A terrible beauty is born."
"You'll have to beat the boys back with a paddle,"
Big Anita says. I smile. Already,
I can see my swaying hips.

# Apartment Hunting with Anita

Only minutes ago, the landlady
with tight curls and a gold cross
told my stepmother, Anita,
this apartment was taken.
Now, she's handing me the key.
I'm 18. Baskin Robbins fired me
for serving too much ice cream
per cone.

I step to the bay window.
Palm trees wave below me.
Half a block away, Anita,
in a new suit, sits in the passenger
side of my mother's old car.
Her black hair shines. I'm wearing
torn jeans. My straw-colored hair
needs brushing. All I had to do
to rent this apartment
was show up in my white skin.

Anita was seeing my dad before
my mother died. Her salsa burns
my throat. She loves large, lime-
colored paper roses. She's beautiful,
with long brown legs. *All her sins.*

She's worked as a hairdresser
at the same shop for 20 years.
She doesn't drop socks on the rug
or burn stews to lava crusts.
Until this moment, I was sure
I was the one to feel sorry for.

I smile at our new landlady.
Already I can see lime roses
in a bottle by the window.

# My Stepmother Kicks Me Out
## Because I'm Not a Virgin

How ironic.
She is yelling, "*Puta!*"
Her black negligee sleeves flap like crow's wings.
She sails my un-mailed letter across the room.
We stare as it lands, an origami bluebird, on her white carpet.
"Falsely accused," I shout. I like to hurl
famous quotes so she will tilt her beautiful head and blink.
Her English is imperfect, but I heard her
perfectly when she once told me
she had been with my dad before my
mother died. Now, I can picture her
snooping in my bedroom, trying to read
my tight handwriting.
In the letter to my East Coast boyfriend,
I thanked him for stepping out of his Chevy in a blizzard
to buy me sanitary napkins. I had just started my period.
In the Chevy, we had watched the snow drape bare trees,
so beautiful to me, a California girl. His pants
stayed zipped, my turtleneck and schoolgirl plaid skirt intact.
The words sanitary napkins and period must have burned
neon-blood red on the thin airmail page.
I want my pajamas, my purse, my *Oxford
Book of English Verse*.
I want anything that is mine.
"Out! *Puta!*"
Her voice is loud. She means it.
"Dad?" I ask.
Dozing in his easy chair, he sighs. She steps
between him and me. Maybe that's why
they call them stepmothers. She shoves me
toward the door, my dead mother's car key in my hand.
Behind me, the front door slams.

# Home Movies

*for my father*

When you were on the skids,
you saw yourself as Ulysses
cruising the wrong way
down Main Street
on your Suzuki motorcycle
at 3 a.m.

You picked fights in bars,
stole kisses from women,
dodged your wife in her
midnight-blue Rambler,
laughed when she aimed
the butcher knife at your heart.

You heard voices.
J. Edgar Hoover confessed
his sins to you. Snakes
swung in your shower.

You sneaked home to me,
your daughter. Your words
big as beach balls: "Never
dreamed I had so many lives."

Nodding in the predawn gloom,
searching for soup, coffee
and your B-12 vitamins,
I was like Penelope,
unraveling all my accomplishments
because you appeared
at my door.

# 501 Valley Drive

*for John*

Chaste in our pajamas,
we held each other
in that knotty pine bedroom
until our wedding in TJ.
Back in our bungalow
on Valley Drive,
after vows,

me, slipping out of my wool dress.
Your skin, smelling of salt water
and lime cologne,
saving me.
Morning coffee, your Marlboros.
Palm tree in a lumpy patio.
We sat under the rusted umbrella.

Your dark blue eyes
matching the cotton of your shirt,
the dark blue ink of your pen
in your long tan fingers
filling out the racing forms.
Horses galloping us
out of our future

# Like Mother, Like Daughter

# Snowing in Tilden Park

The TV weather woman
wasn't born the last time
it snowed in Tilden Park.
But I was. My eyes in the dark
searched for the neon exit sign.

Snow so deep in my head.
Bare dark trees. Green Berkeley
hills tinseled with white.
Death and razors courted me.

I didn't believe plum trees
could burst into bloom.
But they did. I did.
Enemy San Francisco skyscrapers
shrunk to kindly sentinels.

How sweet the strawberries
were that summer of stray dogs
and street songs. Each ripe peach
I bought at Pon's grocery sat
in its own cup of green paper.

Tonight, years later, the black sky pours ice on my head.
My daughter carved her wrist with a razor.
She told me what I once told myself.
"It's not death I crave. Just peace."

My daughter is a small, unreachable figure
disappearing in her snowy glass globe.

At the Korean grocer's on this winter night
I feel the remembered warmth of the peach
that summer of love,
placed in my hand. I pick shiny black
eggplants, Shitake mushrooms

and a globe of egg-white garlic
for my daughter's dinner.

# Hospital Garden

Winter and that hanging judge
in my head. Demons
wore my family's faces,
said I was evil, a witch
hitched to a storm cloud.
Outside the window
of Ward 3 South
it was spring.
One silver Saturday
I earned a hospital pass
to sit in the botanical gardens.
Squat cacti, shaped like paddles.
Military spines.
Brooding saguaros,
with large limbs: the stalking
giants of children's nightmares.
The sun on my back.
Bees.
Ocotillos: tawny ballerinas
with blossoms
the color of menstrual blood.
Butterflies.
Prickly pears elbowing
each other in their square
of tenement soil.
Butter yellow blossoms.
The sun on my back.
Birdsong.
My white legs freckled.
My face turned pink,
a desert poppy.
The hanging judge
in my head
slipped out of his robe
and dozed in the sun.

# The Sounds of Your Leaving

Now, I have the quiet house
I once wished for.
I can hear wind in live oaks,
crows' grumpy *Uh-huhs*,
the autumn comment of toads.

Your dad's shower is a waterfall.
He dries himself with the thin hug
of a towel, and, like you, leaves.

I miss the midnight melody
of your keys in the lock,
the mating call of your ringing phone,
angry women singers roaring
at their mothers and their men.

I wait for your buzz as you,
a Kabuki-hummingbird,
towel on head, avocado mask on face,
dart past. Will the bus driver
who palms your ticket
know the gray air you fill is sacred?

In your room, I rest my face
in your dress, breathe in coconuts
and almonds of your shampoo.
Like the ocean in a cowrie shell,
you've left an echo.

Your laughter, at first small,
unwinds like a slinky
from my belly where you started
to the city where you live.

# The Order of Things

Home from college, she climbs
in the car, squints at my hair.
Her father wants me to look
glamorous like his actress friends.
I wound my hair in sponge rollers
and combed it into a stiff helmet.

I wait for her to tell me
I look stupid. She has always
been my critic-in-residence.
Daughters denigrate their mothers
so they will have the courage
to leave. The order of things.
"I love your hair, Mom," she says.

The car reeks of too sweet hair spray.
Airport palms look like movie trees
on this bright December day.
I streak onto the wrong freeway.
Cars in the next lane zip past.

She sits forward. "We're lost."
Her words anxious puffs of air.
"I want to kill myself. Let's do it together."
She smiles in conspiracy.
"You're not that happy."

Like dove-gray kindling, my fear ignites.
"I don't want you to die," I tell her.
I glance at myself in the car mirror,
a timid woman under a foreign helmet.

She leans against me,
the sweet, small weight of her
an arrow in my bow.
I will become a warrior.
I don't know it yet.

Sunglasses hide my wet eyes.
I'm grateful for a car that runs,
all my credit cards, this black blazer
that makes my shoulders big.
I tell my first lie:
"I know the way home."

# Hanging Up Her Clothes

Last night, she threw her clothes,
books, and nail polish bottles
across the small bedroom
of her college apartment.

This morning, she shrugged into her fuzzy
coat to ride the bus to school.
Her doctor says the risk
of her stepping in front of a bus,
hanging herself or cutting her wrist
is low to moderate.
Going to class will give her confidence.

I clamp the waist band
of a slinky skirt
and slip a blood-red blazer
on a hanger.

I think of all those trips
to her favorite store, Papaya.
A yawning mall mom, I'd find
a chair and shut my eyes.

Now, I caress each skirt, shirt, tank top,
and the glittering rhinestone starfish
my daughter once wore in her hair.

# Putting Out the Fire

Folding my daughter's laundry,
fixing  her "regular" after-
school treat: tortilla, sauce,
and cheddar. The two of us waiting
for her school bus. I didn't know
she was plotting her death.
Her doctor tells us to think of
her Bipolar Disorder as a fire
in her brain. Each time
of sadness or mania adds kindling.
At night in her warm apartment,
we share a futon. Her head rests
on my chest. She is so close.
My breath, gentle on her cheek,
blows out the flame.

# Vigil

"Have Sara arrange my funeral. You'll be too upset.
Besides, you're not good with details."
She studies the kitchen door jamb, the height
of the step ladder, the length of the bathrobe cord
her brother wears over his sweater and jeans.
She is good with details.
"If you promise to travel, really go to Ireland,
my life would mean something."
Her life is a runaway kite I can't wind home.
A kerchief hides her red hair. Her eyes dart.
She looks like one of her ancestors
on the alert for the next pogrom.
The microwave dings. "Nachos," her brother says.
Weak February light brings out the red in his beard,
the worry lines on his forehead.
"Time for *One Life to Live*." I herd my daughter
to the couch, pen her in with the coffee table.
She nibbles cheese, shoves the plate away.
Her brother says, "You have to eat, Habibi."
On the TV screen, Vicki, our favorite character
is wearing red. Outside, rain begins again.
My daughter closes her eyes, leans against her brother.
Over her bent head, her brother and I each take
a small breath. Tired is good.
The doctor said it's the bursts of energy
we need to worry about.
My daughter's head droops. I pour my son tea.
Like the baby she once was, she awakes startled.
She looks around the apartment—a cold dark cave,
then back to the screen where
Vicki is also pouring tea.
"When are the daytime Emmys? Our show will win."
"In May," I say.
"May," she whispers. A promise to herself, and
to that faraway month of flowers.

# Patients in Pajamas

In a rainstorm we drive to K-Mart,
buy one pair of pajamas,
get one free.
We meet each other
in our narrow rooms
and stare at our twin selves.
In matching pastel stripes,
I'm her fellow patient, not her mother.

After my surgery,
she serves me soup and Jell-O.
I make sure she takes her meds,
On the days her tongue swells,
her temperature soars,
I slip a jacket over my pj's,
and rush to the pharmacy.
Rain and wind,

we build a fire in the wood stove,
sit in our stripes, watch
*Pride and Prejudice.*
Like the Bennet women,
we do needlework.
A faux spring January day,
my daughter, in her pajamas
and garden shoes, plants succulents

by our door. I tuck the hems
of pajama legs in rubber boots,
empty compost, cat litter.
We live in the land of the ill,
but this is a life. We put birdseed
in our feeder, write our poems.
Our flannel pajamas grow softer
with each wash.

# What Women Do

## After Charlottesville

I carry my dreams into the day.
White men in hoodies wave
tiki torches, chase me, a Jew—
a woman, and old—down allies,
and neon-lit streets. I'm slower
than the girl I once was, the brick
searing past my ear, the words
"Christ killer" singing the air.
Through the egg wash of morning
mist, I see a finch at the feeder.
The great ones, Tolstoy,
Symborska, say even in times
of war, life stitches wounds.
A peasant buys fish at the market.
A beetle crosses a plaza.
A prodigal cat appears at the door.

# An Iranian Woman Watches the Protest of Neda's Death

"Make up should be for your
husband only," my mother
says in my head. In real life,
she is home in her apartment,
blowing cool air on her second
cup of tea, filling out her grocery list.

"You don't need a clock,
you can tell time by the tasks
she performs," my father always half-
grumbles, half praises.

From the secret pocket of my hooded
black coat, I pluck
a small tube, too big for a bullet,
too small for a gun. I daub color
on dry lips.
Half a block away, a few women,
some young, some my age, shout slogans,
wave posters of Neda.

I promised my mother I wouldn't
come anywhere near here. I tell myself
I will stay on this street. Spoiled olives
drop like bruises from the tree
at the sidewalk.

In this 10 o'clock Saturday sun,
the lipstick is the tentative pink
of a small smudge in a white
apple blossom.

Before Western books were banned,
I bought Brontës and Austens from the book
store with the faded awning.

Those days, I walked to work
in heels, tilted my painted face
like a flower to the sun.

No policeman here to copy
my license plate, shatter
my windshield. I could climb
back in my car, drive by
the protestors, honk my horn,
wave two fingers in a victory V

and speed home to my husband
and son. I pocket my lipstick, walk
toward the women,
one of them in a tight coat,
nervous streaks of eyeliner
like winding streets on her lids.

Two *Basijis*, so young
and not wearing their helmets,
stroll around the corner.
They are laughing, sipping sherbet.
Their truncheons loose in their hands.
They are like my cousin Isar,
who believes women deserve
cut faces, split bones.

I should turn back. On this warm
day, my head is hot under the hood
of my coat. I think of the night
my son was born, my prayer
of thanks that he was not a girl.

One of the men tosses the last
of his sherbet on a poster of Neda,
abandoned on the sidewalk. I slide
behind a tree. I hope the *Basijis*
will rush past.

In my secret pocket, my phone rings.
Rubinstein's sweet piano playing Chopin.
My mother's Saturday call.
It is 11 o'clock.

# Meeting Place

*AP Photo: Saturday, August 9, 2008, The Republic of Georgia*

Chain link fence, a field,
a narrow, wood bench,
shade from an untrimmed tree.
Sparrows still twittering
this August morning.

Maybe they are grandmothers,
wide white arms
in summer house dresses,
open-toed shoes.

The one on the bench in black,
a babushka on her head.

The other, in a red print dress
with English letters.
Maybe, only a moment before,
she had stood, small purse in hand,
gray curls and dress flapping
in the slight breeze.

Maybe the woman in black had smiled,
a story on her lips.

Now, wild ivy in her hair.
The red dress hiked above the knees,
white turnip legs stretched out,
purse near curved fingers.
Blood on her nose and forehead.
Eyes open, as if surprised
by the icy crackle of gun fire.

Her friend sits crying.
Two fresh loaves of bread
on the bench beside her.

# Woman with Shopping Cart
## Sings to the Sea

Glory be to God for shiny things.
Walking the bluffs, the wheels of the cart
leave little trails in dusty soil. A ribbon
of green in gray waves below.
Across the street, a taxi stops by a house
with palms. A lady in velvet, heels clattering,
steers packages and dog. She's in for the night.
I park the cart next to a twisted tree trunk.
Blanket to my shoulders, night not too cold.
Dappled, not shiny. Getting old. I love all things
shiny: globe Christmas ornaments tipped with white
that look like glazed sugar, the glass door knob
I keep in my pocket, gold foil, and silver—
really aluminum, shook dazzling in my hand.
Moon split by clouds. Half sandwich from Delaney's,
so many treasures just trashed away. Music. Pier
with the merry-go-round my father took me to on Sundays.
Now, pastrami and Dijon mustard on my tongue.
Oh Santa Monica, still beautiful.
A girl in Latin class, I looked out the window
at sail boats every Wednesday, doctors cruising
on their day off. Why Wednesdays? Surely harder
to be sick than treat the sick. Dementia. Dolphins
on surfboards.
Hopkins by flashlight. Dappled for sure.
Lights from the fishing boats stipple the sea.

# The Woman in Space 23
### Orange Tree Trailer Park

Better to skimp on food and pay the electric bill
so my daughter won't find me dead,
only my knitted cap peaking above the covers.
Food stamps. Day old bread. Dumpster diving
behind the Cask and Cleaver.
Once a whole lobster. Once I was so hungry
my hand grabbed a banana at the fruit stand.
No security cameras like inside
a market where I see me waddling down the aisle
in my wine-colored pants.
That banana day was a Saturday. Trader Joe's
two blocks down  gave out samples of ravioli
and garlic bread. When Chelsea, next space over,
has her electricity turned off,
she uses my oven. I went on Welfare
when my daughter was born. Only for a year.
Those days you could live on
what you made serving burgers,
selling shoes, even pitching pot holders, picture
frames over the phone. Pacific Blind Products
is what they called it. Wash cloths sewed
by the blind. Once I lived on the street.
My daughter was grown then and didn't know.
I never felt safe to fall asleep.
Two months ago there was a stabbing at our park.
We all try harder now to watch out for each other.
My daughter helped me buy my home. I painted
the trailer egg shell white, yolk trim. I keep it neat.
Tuesdays are busy for Chelsea and me.
Cans and bottles, recyclables. Riches.
When my daughter visits, she sees my red, yellow
and orange nasturtiums. She bends down to sniff
their spicy flowers. "Ma, I'm proud of you,"
she says. "You're doing fine."

# Jane Austen's Desk

Her desk and chair wait in a corner
of the common sitting room
as if she had left a moment before.
The tour guide says: "Miss Austen refused
to have the door's squeak oiled to silence it.
The noise warned her of visitors.
She slid her work under a blotter."

It would be hard to hide stamps
in this narrow desk, never mind chunks
or reams of *Persuasion* and *Emma*.
She wasn't the great Jane Austen then,
just a dependent Aunt Jane, welcoming
a brother's warm fire, a neighbor's
joint of meat.

I can see Miss Jane Austen, pen in hand,
at her desk, dissecting a woman's heart
as if it were her own. The door squeaks.
She swallows a sigh of anger? Regret?
Still in that half-dream, and standing now,
her finger taps mahogany. She steps
to greet a family visitor.

# At the Brontë Parsonage

Outside, the wind and rain
Charlotte and her sisters
made famous. Grave stones
march up the hill to windows
of this high-ceiling room.

Rain drips from my closed
umbrella onto her hardwood
floor. I can almost hear
her father's sermons,
the scratch of Brontë pens.

Five-foot-one, 110 pounds,
I'm an Amazon, a clumsy giant
next to her white dress
on the headless mannequin.

No matter how hard
I could hold my breath,
or suck in my belly,
I would rip those dainty
stitches, pop those buttons.

How did Charlotte, a tiny
candle of a woman, ignite
Jane and Rochester's bonfire,
listen to the sounds of her
sisters' fading breaths?

Slow, small brain,
furry old heart, I lumber
closer, reach to cradle
her dress in my wet,
broad arms.

# The Mothers of the Mentally Ill

She clutches my hand. "I'm glad
it's me. Not you. I was worried
you would lose your daughter."
I cry into her shoulder.
My purse drops.

Evening sun floods the church,
haloes Barbara's dark hair,
turns Jesus on the cross the rose
and gold of Limoges.

She strokes her son's cool forehead,
his tweed jacket, his father's blue tie,
the rosary twined in his fingers.
In his coffin, he looks as if he's smiling,
thinking of his next Coke,
his next cigarette.

Tall candles. Incense.
Perfume from stocks and roses.
Women in dark dresses,
our friends, the mothers we met
in the waiting room, fill the pews.

Barbara's hand. soft as pastry,
under mine. "He wasn't even safe
in the hospital. They tried to heal
him. Killed him instead."

Twilight. A woman plays a hymn
on the piano.
My purse on the carpet starts to hum.
My daughter is calling.
Barbara slides her chair closer
to the coffin.

# Office Hours, 1979

Ten years now, this old VW
has been my office. With its open
face and big hands, my kids'
alarm clock sits like one of them
in passenger's seat, ticking away

my hours from noon to 4.
Steering wheel for a desk, I pencil
in names of characters who have talked
all week in my head.
Part of me is still back home

with my kids, where I can't work,
where walls scream for paint,
where baby sitters take the few
dollars I save from our food allowance
to watch my children.

I sip guilt with my coffee, wish
this artist-me would go away. Through
a bug-stained windshield
I watch a woman named Sunny weed,
plant annuals, edge her lawn.

I can't work in my neighborhood, where
a woman alone in a car is a target.
Here, flowers grow freer than weeds.
Pieces of twisted metal poke through
upholstery, jab my back.

Seconds leak out of me like blood.
The alarm rings. Mother-writer, I think
I may be dying in this rotting car.
It will take me 10 more years
to learn these office hours

are not a death. They are routine
maintenance, the weeding, edging,
and weekly plantings of dreams.

# Spring, after a Long, Cold Berkeley Winter

*for Olivia*

My old four-cylinder Pontiac Tempest climbing
green Berkeley hills. Your fiancé and my father
both in jails down south. Plum trees in bloom.
The latest *New Directions* in our scuffed purses.
Chanting *To a Poor Old Woman*, *Rip Rap*,

*Howl*, we cruise down dark, tree-lined streets
past Van Gogh irises, roses in bloom. One of the ivy-
covered bungalows could be Rexroth's or Ginsberg's.
Ginsberg, wild curls, wild arms, words like waves,
a nervous shepherd directing his flock on Telegraph.

You in a pea-green, yellow-check maternity dress.
The two of us standing in shadows at the curb.
My waitress, your secretary money running out.
Our apartment on Ashby. The oven door that never
closes. The window that never opens. Strawberries

from the co-op. Spiral notebooks with UC Berkeley
on the covers. We wrote all that spring. In love with
William Carlos Williams, his plums, his nasturtiums,
his asphodel, his white space. Our poems, footprints
on the page, we said. Seagull tracks across the sand.

Hair neatly combed, shoes polished, we slid past
Sather Gate, sneaked into the back of Thom Gunn's
poetry class. The real students, girls from good homes,
with hawk-nest hair, in torn blue jeans, were dropping out.
We were slipping in.

# Truants from the Suburbs

> *I now want to make myself as scummy as I can.*
> *Why? I want to be a poet.*
> — Arthur Rimbaud

A waif with dyed blond hair, boots and mini-skirts,
a stolen library copy of *Ariel,*
and a devil's wheel of birth control pills,
I ballooned my dime-store depression
to Plath's helium-sized *every tulip is a spear* despair.
Liv, my pregnant poet/roommate, and I sailed
Rimbaud's drunken boat, his Paris mist our Berkeley drizzle.
We saw altars in garbage, saviors in seaweed,
jewels in muddy gutters. Rimbaud had Verlaine,
we had Wakoski in black leather, riding
with her motorcycle man on rain-slicked
Berkeley streets. The scum in our lives
swam to the top like fat in chicken soup.
Liv's lover in jail for the criminally insane,
my father drunk-pounding on our door.
We read Jung, our bad-assed shadow-selves
stretching out like elongated winter silhouettes.
We wrote rengas at office breaks, villanelles at our shaky
kitchen table. We shivered, taped our broken windows,
placed newspapers in the gap under the front door.
We didn't yet know Rimbaud gave up writing
in rainy Paris to sell coffee beans in sunlit Yemen.

# Moon Dance

*What a fabulous night for a moon dance.*
— Van Morrison

Darkness. The motion lamp clicks on,
haloes a corner of the farm house,
my dog Duffy, sway back, tinker toy legs,
and me, asthmatic in knit cap and parka.
Under my gas mask, I hum,
*The Way You Look Tonight.*
Fred in tux, Ginger in full skirt
Duffy and I swing down the path.
Past the steaming compost,
by the arbor a new light, a new tableau.
Duffy teetering in tall grass, me hunched
in a cough. We rise in the mist.
In our long midnight shadows,
we are dancers in a Degas.
Moonlight in full flood finds us
on the road in plaid. Casey, the spaniel,
and coyotes in the grove chorus:
*Go home with Bonnie Jean.*
Duffy's tail wags. He's Gene in kilts.
I'm Cyd in heels.
We dance the hills of Brigadoon.
The barn owl leaves the wire.
Moon behind a thunder cloud.
Rain begins again. Just past midnight.
Already Gonzales's crazy roster crows.

# I Find Po Chu-I in the Mountains

at the Pine Tree Market. In a Padres baseball cap,
he buys Oreos and chili-flavored chips.
"Are you up for poetry week?" I ask.
"I live here." And he's out the door, bells jingling
behind him.

I check scattered mailboxes, lonely cabins.
I find Po Chu-I by a stream. He sits on a stone wall,
his feet in purple myrtle. "How do you live here
all year alone? And write? I can't do it."
He wraps his arm coach-style around my shoulder:
"Stay within yourself."

No words all day. The narrow computer screen
a closing eye. I stumble into yellow twilight.
Past a boulder, I find Po Chu-I under the pines.
He sings his poems to rabbits and trees.

In my cabin, the whirring fan, a solitary dancer.
Pencil in hand, I stand on my balcony,
read to startled jays.

# Reading Po Chu-I on a Rainy Night,
## I Dance Sometimes

My belly too full, the night late,
I read Po Chu' I, who after
collecting taxes in autumn
from peasants he loved,
drank too much wine
and danced sometimes.

My own shopping cart full,
I give a quarter
to a woman with whiskey
on her breath, a dusty black
poodle, an old rag coat,
and empty cans in her cart
on a cold Saturday night.
Sometimes I drink too much
wine and dance.

Men far from their home
in Mexico live next to me
in shacks, with cloths for
windows, and rain leaking in.
They pick avocados
I lace with lime and cilantro.
I drink too much wine
and dance sometimes.

Dawn to dark,
young girls in Viet Nam,
necks curled like old women,
straw cutting their fingers,
weave beach mats
I sit on in summer.
Sometimes I drink too much
wine and dance.

# Gladiators' Houses in Ruins
## by the Roman Coliseum

*for Colin Kaepernick*

Half a wall still standing. Ecru
humps of Roman concrete—quick-
lime, water, volcanic ash—glitter
in the rain. Poor boys, former
slaves lived here. Clothed. Fed.
Celebrated with laurel leaves.
Told not to speak.

Mouths shut like boarded houses.
Words lost in ruins,
lost in the fields of rubble
where gladiators once lived.

Their deaths predictable. Eyes
squinting through bronze grids.
Limbs, lungs, exposed like glass
windows. Half a wall still standing.
Poppies red as blood in bloom.

# The New Drug

*for Elbia*

She says, "I want a tattoo.
A vine with snail flowers
along the stitches, a sassy
elephant where my breast
used to be."

Her wooden spoon poised
like a spear, we stand and wait
at the stove for the water
for rice to boil.

On the kitchen radio,
news of another
cancer drug.

She is almost my sister-wife,
married my first husband,
cared for him in a way
I never could.

She is the one who tells
me the truth
when no one else will,
the one who went with me
the day I had to pick out
my father's coffin.

She straightens her shoulders,
sets the spoon down,
turns the stove's knob.
Under a saucepan the circle
of orange fades slowly to gray.

She pours coffee into mugs
leads me out to her backyard
where we will sit for awhile
in a slice of sunlight
on this winter afternoon.

# Virginia's Boots

Picking the last cherry tomatoes
dumping orange peels and old lettuce
in my compost bin
I can still see her
the way she was her last cold winter
standing in her yard, hands on blue-jeaned hips
boot heels digging in mud
a straw hat hiding chemo-thinned hair
telling me, "That shredder
was the best investment I ever made."
In her yard, Aggie, the goat, ate branches.
Chicken scraps went to cats.
Even bones were ground
for soup or compost.

While we were feeding apples to horses
one gray day last autumn
I told her, "The worst curse
of getting older is seeing your friends die."
Her green eyes blinked, disappointed:
"Curses are a waste."
Then, she looked up through bare trees
and scanned the sky for geese.

Now I wear her cowboy boots
in my yard.
They're tan like our soil
thick with three-inch heels.
I dig my toes through fleece,
stretch my feet in tight leather.
Someday these boots will fit.

# Lentil Soup

*for Lisa*

A coyote calls to its kin.
A rabbit shifts under a porch light.
Lizards, coyotes, hummingbirds,
foxes—your daughter, Natalie,
rescued, nursed them all.
It is my turn, now, Lisa.
I've simmered curry, garlic,
lentils, celery, bay leaf, hot cayenne,
on this early summer night,
two days past the solstice,
this odd, sacred window
between your daughter's death,
and the celebration of her life.
For 23 years, you've brought cornbread,
bird seeds, sweet peas
to my front door.
Two nights ago, you gripped
the nurse's pen,
and asked to sign away
Natalie's eyes,
her still beating heart.
Wind rattles frail windows.
The season turning,
moon going down.
My turn to search for words
I don't have. Only carrots
and cayenne jarred now
with lentils in glistening glass.
A woodpecker knocks
at the front door, taps at a hole
in the door frame,
retrieving an acorn he stored
last fall for this summer night.

# What Women Do

Red-headed bank teller Patsy, in a dress
and heels, bugles, *Poppies, lupines,* tugs me
into a twilight of new green leaves and sweet sage.
Young Lisa, scent of lavender she pruned this morning
still on her hands, says, *Anna hummingbirds*, wraps
a lilac shawl around my perennial black turtleneck.
My friends pretend not to notice dark jump ropes
under my eyes or the narrow squint of the shell-shocked.
Mia, menopausal in peony-pink sweats, guides
me on the trail of her favorite beach. Pewter waves
thundering, I pray my daughter will live. White-haired
Miss Arleen, in pearls and an old money-green linen dress,
braves Roberto's sawdust floor, feeds me fish tacos.
Over the blare of mariachi trumpets, she covers my hand
with hers, tells me: *New meds will kick in.* I want
to ignore the insistent spring. My next door neighbor
master-gardener Linda, in dirt-spattered jeans, dusty clogs,
serves me tea, pots succulents for my patio.

# Her Breasts Still Full of Milk

Out my kitchen window, my daughter
sits under our live oak, feeds her baby
girl, Elana, which means "oak tree"

in Hebrew. The scene so painterly.
My daughter, with red hair, wearing
a Renoir blue dress. The dog, Sunny,
buff colored like our soil, by her side.

I scour a pot for our stew. On TV,
an announcer says a Border Agent
took a breast-feeding baby from

a mother seeking asylum. The border
50 miles away, and I so helpless.
My fingers burn under water
running hot too long. I am white
and safe here in America.

My grandfather escaped the Cossacks
a century ago.
Sometimes I rock Elana.
Her skin on my skin, her sighs,
her friar fringe of hair.

I think of my great grandmother
holding my grandfather, an infant
in her arms, when the soldiers came.

I slice carrots and picture the mother
with her baby at her breast. She stands
tired under the icy fluorescent light
of the detention center. The agent
with thick fingers, stiff uniform, hot

breath on the mother's face,
grabs her child from her grasp.
The feel of her baby's wet-
soft mouth still on her nipples.
The sweet weight of her baby
gone from her arms.
Her breasts still full of milk.

# Mothers and Sons

# The News

*for Danny*

He said yes, you—smaller than a lima bean—
were growing inside me. The doctor,
a short Italian man with glasses, was smiling.
The scale from the trickster universe, so heavy
on the bad side—my dead mother,
my gutter-drunk dad—tipped wildly.
The belly I once girdled and bound
was expanding now, a pool for you
little floating olive.
Even as I changed from my paper gown
to my shop-girl skirt and plain blouse,
I noted my browning nipples.
A bird hummed in my head. My fingers
turned to fruits, guavas, fuzzy kiwis,
and pomegranates.

# How You Began

*after Dawson Young*

The front of the year.
Your father and I.
A soft night in a little
back house on Raymond.

Neighbor children—Susie,
Karen, Steve—safe in bed
for the night.

A love song in Spanish
from the cottage across
the street. Enrique's
cigarette glowing
under the avocado tree.

Love, ripe like the oranges,
lanterns in the trees.
You were made in Ocean Park
at the beginning of the year.

The sea, a skein of gold
five city blocks away
under a full moon.

The trolley with lights
and bells
trundling up the boardwalk.

Women in babushkas,
men in prayer shawls.
Bonfires on the beach.

Ukuleles and bongos.
Poets and junkies seeing
magic in the flames.

You began in the bedroom
with the slanted roof, yellow
Oxalis blooming at the door.

# Proposal

*for my son, Danny*

The maid invited me
into the breakfast room
of your father's home.

Your grandmother, her life
peeling away, sat like
a small onion in her wheelchair.

"Our doctor will give you
an abortion. Just say
you're mentally ill,

an unfit mother."
I placed my hand over my belly.
Danny, you were a fiery hub

that kept me spinning.
I was hot iron, the wheel
of a chariot rolling us both

through that great house
onto the cool grass where
even a robin poking for worms

looked bereft.
My scuffed sandals left tracks
on freshly mown lawn.

# The Guides

*for my son, Danny*

The summer I walked
the edge of Lake Sacagawea
you hummed inside of me.
Unwed, I was part mama tiger
with a machete, part little-girl-lost,
attacked by wolves.

My two aunts, women
in their 50s then, took us in.
Fluttering Hazel, a sweet white witch,
brewed herbal tea, and poured
faithful mugs of Postum.
Kay hitched up her Daddy's pants

over her widening hips.
With a hammer she could make sing,
she plumbed and patched
the old family home. Cigarette dangling,
and sipping whiskey, she told me,
"Any family member in trouble

has a home here."
Kay and Hazel hauled rocks
from the Toutle River,
scattered stones through thick reeds,
and carved a path to the warm house
for you and me.

# The House on Dover Street

I quoted poetry to Aunt Kay while she fried
the Friday-night fish. Aunt Hazel went to Mass every morning.
She never said the words "unwed" or "sin."

Eight months pregnant, I slept on their fold-out
couch. Aunt Kay sat in her "Holey chair."
Hazel perched on the rocker.

They whispered over me when they thought
I was asleep. "She's not eating enough."
"She needs another blanket."

My aunts stayed up late with Johnny Carson,
got up early with their Postum. Kay, a school janitor.
Hazel, a bookkeeper for Sherick's grocery.

I hung my summer sweater in the dark hallway.
The Northwest smell of old wood warmed by a radiator
in winter, never drying out in fleeting summer sun.

Bursting out of my plaid maternity dress,
making plans for my child, I walked along
the Longview slough, came back to Dover Street.

I was the daughter of their junkman brother,
the first to leave this house. Red-headed,
left-handed, he was the one they loved the most.

# Plenty

*for Danny*

My first writing teacher told us,
"When a story fails, laugh and say,
*There's plenty more where that came from."*
I thought she was mad.
My tortoise-mind crawled
across a desert where little bloomed.
But even deserts can surprise.
On hot, dry nights, a story I wrestled with
20 years ago will wake me by whispering,
"This is how I should end."
In the rainy season, stories, poems,
whole books, flash and wink in the floods.

# Loving Tiffany

My 7-year-old son
wore a dress.
His favorite doll, Tiffany,
had dyed blond hair,
a skimpy gold skirt,
white Go-Go boots.

I was sure my son wanted to be Tiffany.
I was sure I didn't want him to be Tiffany,
EVER.
How could my son love this Las Vegas
show girl of a doll
when men measured my worth

by the size of my breasts,
when my cute femaleness had cost me jobs
and income? I was letting my Summer Blond
hair grow out, packing up my boots and miniskirts.
I was righteous WOMAN kicking into HER jeans.

I dreamed of tearing Tiffany apart,
burying bits of her in my garden,
an arm and gold bracelet in the roses,
a kneecap in the onions,
but I knew another Tiffany would appear.
I sent my son to a therapist.

"Make him like himself," I said.
She said I was a domineering mom.
He needed strong, successful, male role models:
Martin Luther King, JFK, Cesar Chavez.

There was no more Tiffany.
There was an absence,
an abalone shell without the muscled flesh.
When I whispered, "I love you,"
my son did not believe me
because he knew I did not love Tiffany.

My son, a shadow teen, lived
a monk's life. In our small town,
the TV repairman was the leader of the Klan
and ran for Congress. My son escaped
the notice of the skinheads. Sometimes I wished
for Tiffany,

but if she appeared, I would aim
for her knees. Now, my son, the reader
of men's biographies,
is an AIDS activist,
a pink prom dress hangs in his closet.
Dresses hang again in my closet too.

To love my son, I had to cherish
the showoff summer blond in me.
Now my wide androgynous arms
embrace us all, Martin Luther King,
Cesar Chavez, me and my mini-dress
and Go-Go boots,

my 7-year-old son
wearing a prom dress,
and Tiffany, bright and lurid,
in her gold fringe.

# The Lake of Swans

*for Rudy Galindo*

>*(The first openly gay male ice skater and the first Mexican-American to win the United States Figure Skating Championship, San Jose, 1996)*

My sister Laura tells me I must skate
this one last time. My blades hiss and sputter.
The rink, my lake of swans.

The judges say I am the wrong color.
Brown men cut asparagus
by day, disappear like dry leaves
by night. I wear black ruffles and twirl.

The judges say I am too light on my feet.
How light is too light?
Where is that cruel line where grace
becomes too sweet?

The judges say I don't attack like a man.
I glide. I float. Black feathers
mate the ice.

I dance. I sing. I soar
with that other miscast princess
Peter Tchaikovsky,
whose music kept my trailer walls
from closing in,
whose music sweetened the squeals of tires,
the quarrels of the poor.

Ice cool at my feet, ice cruel at my feet.
I hear the burble of the IV, feel the chill
of last words. Lord, why am I, skinny
Rudy Galindo, still here? Still skating?
I see the graves. The ice is a grave.
I want to fall in, into the arms of the ones
I miss and love.

My brother and two coaches dead from AIDS.
My father dead.
Hands warm my shoulders.
My coaches and my brother blow hot sweet air
on my ankles and knees.

I lift above the ice and fly
I twirl     and twirl     and twirl.
My father sits below me in his old truck.
How hard he worked to keep me in skates.
The music of that other swan calls me home.
Spinning, an audacious bird, I am beautiful.
Faces in the crowd, the flags swirl to rainbows.
Even the judges are on their feet.
My father's arms reach for me.
I glide down to the ice to him. The ice
is not a grave. It is a gate.

# On the Anniversary

*October 12*

In Wyoming twilight, a cyclist saw a scarecrow
tied to a wooden split-rail fence. Not a scarecrow.
Matthew Shepard. Bruised. Beaten. Left to die.
His skull crushed. His blood-caked face washed by tears.

On this anniversary of Matthew Shepard's death,
I try to read, sip tea, count my valley's few stars.
No sleep. My son's would-be killers
could be prowling San Francisco streets tonight.

Broad shouldered football players. Thick jackets.
Tourists from the Midwest. Careful to walk
a few feet from each other. They have been drinking.
Later tonight they will have to share a hotel room

in this expensive city. A bump of an elbow,
a brush of a hand, could be misunderstood.
Mist blows in from the bay.
They tell each other it is girls they like. Girls.

They are nothing like my son with his pretty face and long hair.
Humming to himself, he is coming home
late from teaching.

He wears the pink shirt and tie we bought him.
His light footsteps quicken.
Their footsteps echo his. Their beery breath burn
the back of his neck.

# Wigwam

Tuxedo wars.
My son disinvites
my husband
from his wedding.

I complained
to one about the other
and arranged the kindling
for this fire.
Spring,
letters, hot knives,
sizzle in mailboxes.
I plant beans.
Vines climb string
between bamboo stakes.

August, my sons
no longer welcome
in our home.
The wigwam is a lush
triangle.

I pick buckets
of Kentucky Wonders
for neighbors.
Late fall, leaves yellow.
Silent November,
it's my turn to climb.
Arms aching,
I slice branches,
strip the wigwam.

Three gray poles
tied at the top
with kitchen string
lean together
and face the winter sky.

# Seen from the Hayes Street Bus

Next to me, a woman
with bok choy.

Out the window,
the clang of rush hour.

Cable cars.
Little fires burn and die
on wires overhead.

One pink hibiscus streak
in a darkening sky.

Tall houses and shops
hunch in overcoats
of fog.

A pot of geraniums
on a stoop.

Three stone steps
lead to my son's flat.
A light in the bay window.

The Hayes Street bus
tilts up the hill,

carries me to the dark hump
of the park.

# My Son Calls on My Birthday to Say He Bought His First House

He says he can't wait for the rainy season,
and the ping of drops

on the aluminum roof
of his new patio.

The sound will remind him of the rain
beating on our old tin shed at home.

His words, a gift.
In this hot ranch house—

where he sat on the horsehair couch,
in what he called *the interrogation room,*

and I asked him: *Where were you?
How could you? Why did you?*

—he found comfort
in the heartbeat of rain.

"Stone fireplace in the master
 bedroom," he is saying.

I picture him in his new home.
His wife, already asleep,

her sunrise of gold hair
on their pillow.

The tap dance of rain
on the patio roof.

# On the Eve of Your 39th Birthday

*for Jonathan*

After you've put your sons to bed,
turned on their moon night light,
you walk the dog.

Out in the cold,
your breath shoots wisps of air
ahead of you.

Bailey, the terrier, strains
against her harness, snarls
at every big dog on the block.

You like these winter nights:
warm jacket, an old song
in your headphones.

Venus and Jupiter look like two eyes
above the frown of a crescent moon.
This thirty-eighth year just ending

has been a tug on an old leash
back to the past. So much you
wish you could remember:

The name of the girl with blue eyes
in 7th grade, the color of the front door
of the house on Walnut.

Time is speeding up like those cars
with wings in your sons' cartoons.
Fog washes over the face in the sky.

Today's newspaper says, in the Asian
sky, the crescent moon
was a smile.

You turn the corner to home.
Mist shines on the new blue paint
of your almost classic car.

# House in Summer

*for my children*

I can't wish you back to this house
with narrow rooms.
Each of us walking through, blocking
the other.

Doors that open only with complaint.
Windows stuck half way up their tracks.
Carpets stained from pets long gone.

I can't wish you back here to this house
that shakes with every tiptoe. Too hot
in summer, too cold in winter. A pantry
never quite full.

I can't wish you here, not even on this
summer night sweet with jasmine.
Crickets sing outside
your old cracked windows.
A slice of moon captured in the glass.

# We Sit Up Half the Night

looking at old photos. Pictures scatter
on the table, slip between couch cushions,
fall off of arm rests. One photo of my husband
and me on his parents' patio, sons on our laps,
our VW in the drive. Before the divorce.

A second: Our youngest, age 7,
hair in his eyes. He's on a skateboard
in his dad's studio apartment. Our oldest hiding
behind a book with a winged creature on the cover.
A baseball diamond I don't recognize.

The boys were Yankees that year. My striped sundress
that looked like a deli awning. Way past midnight,
we slide the photos back in manila envelopes, drink
hot chocolate, eat the last slices of birthday cake. Too tired
to drive home I sleep in my grandson's room.

The teddy bear clock ticks. His car bed drives me
through jigsaw puzzles of dreams. I wake to Saturday
cartoons. In my daughter-in-law's pajamas, I tiptoe
past my oldest son, ex-husband, ex-brother-in-law,
on couches under gray blankets.

Over Cheerios and juice, my youngest says,
"Let's make copies of the photos." I grab my purse,
sit in the passenger seat of the van. My ex driving.
Tan hands on the wheel. Sons in back. The four of us
alone together for the first time in 33 years.

I almost whisper: "Remember our car game? Captain
and Co-Pilot and their VIP passengers, Big Cheese and Little
Cheese." I say nothing. Morning traffic moves us along
past parents with baby strollers, and boys in blue and white
uniforms playing baseball in the park.

# For My Son on His Divorce

Four hundred miles from you,
I walk this beach you
love. High tides chase
fisherman up the sand.
A sign reads, *Danger.*
*Intermittent waves*
*of unusual size and force.*
*Swimming unsafe.*

Once, even as I bent in rocky
tide pools to octopus and eel,
you were warm
in a bundle on my back.

Here, in Pacifica, gulls fly
over cliffs to the safety of town.
Cormorants and pelicans
hunker in rocks,
lose their reflections
in the sliding sea.

I pretend you left your troubles
in a pocket on shore.
Hooded, in a wet suit,
booties and fins,
you swim in smooth water
past breaking waves.
I pretend the waves
unfold quietly as lace.

# Family

# Famous Flexible Straws

My father looks up from his meatloaf.
His muddy boots sit in the laundry room.
He shoveled broken dishes, wet clay all day.
"Tell me again about Bobby's sister."
His way of asking for a pep talk.
"She had trouble drinking her milk,
so she bent the straw." My father nods.
He's thinking that's why Bobby's father
drives a Lincoln and moved to 14th Street,
across from the founder of Lear Jets
and the car radio.

My father has a beat-up pick-up.
He hates ritzy Santa Monica.
Our last Brownie trip, we rode horses
at Joel McCrea's ranch.
"The Flexible Straw," my father sighs, walking
to the fridge for his second beer.
No one wants his lawnmower-leaf-
sweeper or his automatic egg-sheller.

He will work half the night in his shop
perfecting a new conveyer belt.
Tomorrow in Brownies, when
I eat Mrs. Lear's chocolate chip cookies,
my father at California China will wear
his rain hat. His hands on the shovel
will turn blue.

# Carlos Called to Tell My Mother Her Husband Was a Cheating Dog

My father, his work boots in his closet,
at rest, at last.
My stepmother, her black mourning dress,
slit at the knee, keening over my father,
lying in his satin lined coffin.
Men, including the broad-shouldered
realtor with a cowboy smile, Lee,
the one I'm sure will be her next spouse,
vie to comfort her.

No shoulder pat of comfort for me from Carlos,
tall, neat, shiny shoes, shiny hair,
my current stepbrother.
He sits next to me and hands me Scotch,
my first, that attacks my tongue
like porcupine quills.

Glancing at the coffin, Carlos tells me he once
called my mother to rat on my father and his mom.
When he heard Mom in her low-pitch voice
doing the family's Groucho joke:
"Hello, I must be going," he hung up.

If he had told her his story
my mother may have believed him.
Receiver heavy in her hand,
she would have gazed at her heart-shaped face
in the mirror above the phone,
heard the rats scratching behind our walls.

# Breakfast at Starbucks

The young barista in his crisp white shirt
squirts whip cream on my latte.
I yawn, tired from my long night drive.
Something familiar about his mild eyes.
Red hair. Narrow farmer's face. Small
bump on his nose. And now I'm staring.
He is my father alive again, reborn
in this sleepy beach town. Cub Scouts,
high school ball, all veering to now,
this morning, this meeting. "You left me,"
I whisper.

The barista slides the cup on the counter,
calls my name. His voice tender,
as if he had chosen the name himself.
"Careful. It's hot." His fingers brush mine.
"Have a good day," he says.
He is so young, so full of good intentions.
His life an uncracked egg. I sip the sweet
brew he made especially for me.

# Reading Sexton's *The Black Art* on our Anniversary

> *But when we (writers) marry*
> *the children leave in disgust:*
> *There is too much food and no one left*
> *to eat up all the weird abundance.*
> — Anne Sexton

*for Bill*

We missed doom by a footpath,
a nuance, a lucky turn.
Love sneaked in under
doorways, caught us tipping
our hats at the mirror.
A nod, a smile, and our fights—
not us—folded their shirts
and left.
A sage-filled hillside kitchen,
the September light on our woodpile,
simmered the watery broth of every day
to a rich soup.
Our children peeked through windows,
thought, "Maybe it is safe."
They stepped in, and paused
at the door on leaving.
The abundance we began with,
the feast that let no one else in,
became as hospitable as cheese.

# Gardenias

> *She'll wear a gardenia and I'll be there.*
> *The Girl that I Marry*     — Irving Berlin

Gene Autry sings, *Old soldiers never die,*
*they just fade away.*
When my cousin Wendy lies, her eyes blink.
Her eyes blink all the time,
snakes pouring from her mouth.
If I could climb on the roof, I could see
everything—sea lions, ships.
My mother says she hates buying my T-shirts
in size chubby.
The apple tree is my safe place.
Red star on the Christmas tree.
My father doesn't come home until after I'm asleep.

I make perfume from orange blossoms.
I'll wear a gardenia and *he* will marry me.
I fall out of the apple tree.
My arm in a sling all summer.
I climb the roof. No sea or ships. Only Tommy next door
beating rugs with a broom.
Wendy says when her parents go into their bedroom
they take their clothes off. *Snakes.*
I throw out orange blossom perfume—
nasty on my closet shelf.
The red Christmas star—phony plastic I could crush in my hand.

Bobby, the smartest boy in Latin class,
wears an army uniform.
He doesn't really die in Vietnam.
He sings in my dreams: *amo, amas, amat.*
I wear a gardenia and marry John.
Wendy sends me a negligee.
John and I fall out of love.
My heart in a sling all summer.

I marry Bill a soldier back from Vietnam.
We live on a ranch with avocados.
Our daughter makes perfume
from orange blossoms.

Bill and I plant an apple tree.
My daughter's friend, Omar, is sent to Iraq.
Her heart in a sling all summer.
We climb the roof, see a family of snakes
curled in a ravine below us.
Wendy sends me e-mails from England.
My daughter falls in love. Her boyfriend
grows gardenias. Perfume every day.
Bill's dead buddies sing in his dreams.
Our grandson finds his chubby toes.
Christmas, I look all over town,
for a red plastic star.

# After an Argument

Words so hot and wild.
Devil winds blew shingles
off our roof.
Apron flying, I ran from the house.
I expected sheets of red flame
marching up our hill.
Only a squirrel in dark chaparral
and an empty snail shell,
bone white in the grass.
The bird feeder you gave me
last birthday swung wildly,
spilled seeds into open hands
of leaves.
The wind hushed.
Moon in the birdbath.
Cassiopeia, whom you love,
hung her head in the night sky.

# Pillows
*for Bill*

My rented cabin closed up
all day. My pillow from home
fire on my back. Windows,
doors open.

Our first bedroom,
that knotty pine cathedral,
the sweet salt and yeast of us.
My body opening, a surprise

like the lipped fruit of a saguaro.

I sit outside on the balcony,
floating like a ship in the pines,
eat spicy spinach with a plastic fork.

Maybe you are resting on the pillow
that is the mate of mine.

A gray squirrel watches me.
I sip ice water. Another hour
until the room cools enough
for sleep.

Maybe you are in your studio tonight.
Your notes from the saxophone
settling on our new green figs.

Here the moon almost full,
curls into the curve of a pine.

# The Nights I Called

Her cat face lit by the quickly muted TV, she slid
her teeth in her mouth, asked, *You couldn't pick
up a phone before now?* Her dead, our dead,
framed in yellowing mats on the wall. I told her,
my grandmother who raised me, I was busy:
greasy dishes, children's homework.
My infrequent calls a slim, sharp, apple corer of
a knife, my silence, a reply to some small assault.
All the nights I didn't call, I pictured her in her night-
gown, her long hair unpinned, needlepoint placed
next to her plate of grapefruit. She sighed,
punched off the TV. *Winter nights so long,*
she used to say. My own nights stretch a hole
in an un-darned sock. My cell phone silent on
an end table. My son busy: work, his children's music, soccer,
karate. I unpin my long hair,
listen to a toad's grumpy wish for rain.
My grandmother's phone number sings
in dry wind.

# The Tree of White Peaches

My grandmother and I,
like two wily alley cats,
not sure why they survived,

filled paper bags
with pink-skinned
fleshy white fruit.

Each spring, the tree
of white peaches grew fat
with leaves and fruit.

On summer nights,
we sat in wicker chairs.
spooning peaches

and vanilla cream,
two cats licking
the last dollop,
our empty house settling
behind us.

The tree: gnarled, top-heavy,
like her. She'd cry
to white blossoms,
*you came back to life.*

Her daughters in their Pageboys,
with literary books and dim husbands,
still dead.

# Visitors

In my daughter's house
after her stroke,
our whispers and tiptoes
are as loud as the slam
of the oven door,

the whistle
of an outraged
tea kettle.

"Where does she keep
the can opener,
the mustard?" we ask.

She's not allowed
to move without us.

We camp outside
her bedroom door,
listen for the rustle
of sheets,

her wobbly, uncertain
steps.

Her father watches
golf on TV. I spill sauce
on her clean stove.

Her house no longer hers.
She almost wasn't ours.

# My Daughter's Breath

You wait in a room with soft couches.
Families clumped in herds, telling stories.
Your daughter down the hall in ICU.
Tubes like eels in her nose and throat.

In the cafeteria you glance at the man
you call Dr. Happy. The man who whistles
on his rounds. The man who told you
your daughter might not come back.
The man bent over his macaroni
pretending he doesn't see you.

Your daughter sleeps small as a locket
in her foamy hospital bed.

Nights you are sure a fox in a nurse's
cap sidles into rooms, steals breaths
and wishes, pours them in a cup
to feed her young.

You bend down to kiss your daughter
good night. Her breath settles
like a pebble in a creek.

You ride the aerial tram back to the room
where you're staying. The tram above
the city dips you down to the dark river,
tilts you up to windy stars.

# Here at the Border
## of Some Country I Don't Know

A skinny nurse, her voice the click of an ice
pick, says my daughter lost 50 percent
of her cognitive ability. The surgeon tells me
neurons can carve new paths through
a damaged brain. I picture a girl scout
with heavy shoes, binoculars, tramping

through ragged brush. My jeans two sizes
too large, my sneakers flaking, a crone in a peaked
turquoise hat, I walk in the rainy cold Portland
summer three miles toward where the city map
claims a Safeway store. Next to peeling
Victorian homes, roses with gray splotches climb

telephone poles, wisteria creeps to roof tops.
I step past railroad tracks onto a street with jack-
hammers, snorting trucks, orange cranes with
dragon's teeth. In a grimy window I see my face.
All hollows. At an indoor café, women in cotton
dresses sip white wine. A strip of sole falls

from my shoe. I pick it, crinkly as shed snake skin,
off the patch of grass. An umbrella at a produce
stand fights wind and slicing rain. I scoop
blueberries into one bag, strawberries into another.
My daughter will be able to sip her favorite
soy milk smoothies through a straw.

# Four Weeks after Her Stroke

my daughter colors her eyelids gold.
We had been suspended, her father,
brothers and I, in the egg-shaped,
metallic, aerial tram, we rode each day
to the hospital. Her brain was bleeding.
Her right side was weak. The tram dangled us
over the city and river. We floated, tilted
on a lake of clouds, helpless as a mouse
in an owl's talons.

Her surgeon whispered she would live.
We were dropped in her tiny living room,
down to the loam of her carpet,
we blinked at each other
and at the salt and pepper shakers
on the table.

July has been dropped from our calendar.
Back to school ads, sneakers with pink laces
on TV. Days are shorter. The maroon hollyhock
we saw our first day here has shut its eyes.
We are opening ours.

We hear her voice, halting at first,
stronger each day, like the adolescent jay
on her front porch, who tilts its head
and listens to its own small screech
growing louder against afternoon traffic.

She has thrown away her cane. She steps
one foot in front of the other down the stairs.

We sit at the dinner table. She can lift
and hold a fork now, quote from *Soap Dish*:
"I've had a rare case of brake fluid."
Her gold eyelids glitter in the evening sun.

# Portland Report

Red hair flowing, a nightgown
with roses, my daughter is a house-
bound wood nymph. If she tries
to stand, she will fall. The wound
in her brain will open. Outside
it is summer, June days long and lazy.

A forest of bamboo,
ferns the size of sturdy 6-year-olds.
Cottage flowers feasting
on rain water, decaying leaves.
Hollyhocks, roses climb
porch stairs. Her father, brothers
and I, camp in her small

college apartment, take turns
at her bedside. We watch the five-
hour version of *Pride and Prejudice*
and soap operas soon to be cancelled.
Her oldest brother names her cane
*Erica*. Outside, girls with vanilla
legs stroll on leafy sidewalks.

My daughter lies down Roman style
on the couch. Her brother washes her hair.
1200 miles south, our friend
feeds our cats. Lisa says our tomatoes
are the size of quarters. One cat crawls
out from under the bed. Green eyes
blink at her. Here, Fourth of July rockets

flash over the Willamette. Starlings
and squirrels feast on cherries.
My daughter takes her first step
with Erica. Her first shower,
a shower stool for support.
We hover outside the bathroom

door, listen to the drizzle of water
on her skin, her unsteady step
as she moves from shower stool to chair.
Her father bakes Eggplant Parmesan,
serves red wine. This could be Tuscany,
sun slanting through blinds,
the family bent over linguini.

Her oldest brother, in a striped shirt
and straw hat teaching her how to hold
a fork. One morning, she wakes up,
asks for a pen and the *Norton Anthology
of Poetry*. Out the window, hydrangeas
big as Kentucky Derby hats. She holds
Erica Cane with one hand, the stair

rail with the other. She counts and climbs
down 16 stairs. Nights shorter now,
her younger brother flies home to his wife
and sons. A squirrel nibbles the last
of the cherries. Her father beside her,
flanked by her older brother, she says
she says she doesn't need her cane.

Late summer breeze from the Willamette,
she dodges a crack in the sidewalk,
takes small steps down South Kelly
Avenue, fallen maple leaves at her feet,
toward day lilies blooming
at the corner of South Curry Street
where some day she will turn.

# Fig Bars

My husband, daughter and I
sit on the bed. Outside, smoke
and ash. On TV, families south
of here pack vans with photos
and pets. Two years ago,
our daughter tried to kill herself.
Today is her birthday.
She writes, *cat carrier, dog leash.*
While we still have electricity
my husband bakes fig bars,

our daughter's favorite,
from fruit he picked two
Septembers ago,
then froze and all but forgot.
Our old wood ranch house,
on the edge of a ravine,
a welcome mat for fire,
smells of cinnamon.
Back in the bedroom,
the three of us huddle,

chew sticky fig bars,
ink in letters
in the crossword,
as if this were a normal Sunday.
As if birds always leave our valley.
Smoke brings an early dusk.
We switch TV channels
from the Woody Allen movie to the news.
The fire now 20 miles away.

The threat we accepted
when we moved here
a quarter century ago
before our daughter was born.
The danger is normal,
we tell her, happy to reassure.
She adds *old photos* to her list.
My husband and I share a smile.
We will watch the skies all night
in case the wind shifts.

# Reading Poetry in Portland

*for my father*

I never thanked you
for my drowsy afternoons
reading Keats and Shelley
the scent of orange blossoms
in a cloudless sky.
Clean pages in my hands,
decades after you've gone
I recite a poem about you at 14
working in the Longview mill.
Weedy grasses by the slough.
the stink of the pulp. Little time
for you to read Edgar Allen Poe,
Walt Whitman under Douglas firs.
In the faces here in the audience,
I see you as a boy, red hair freckles
waiting your turn for the borrowed
shoes to wear to Mass.
Loving the poetic lilt
of the Latin Mass
until the morning
your friend drowned.
You wanted the priest to speak
in English, tell you why
you should still believe
as you sat on the stiff-backed pew
and listened for the whistle,
the canticle of the train
carrying cut lumber
and pulp, those ghosts
of trees you loved, out of town.

# Lessons from the Chaparral

# Father Seahorse

floats, bows and bobs,
births dozens of tiny seahorses,
small replicas of the patriarch,
sailing sideways and upwards
like bubbles from a child's wand.
How happy the seahorses are
to be alive, like wind-blown lettuce,
seeded from Matthew's garden,
now sprouting through a crack
in his beach town sidewalk,
like the injured finch that Lisa
nursed and watched fly
into the yellow-throated sky,
or you, Susan, stage-4 cancer,
leaning on your walker,
snapping photos of roses
and French chandeliers.

# Eve's Task

Once you've dipped
your hand in the pond,
slid your finger under
a moth,
you must sit
in the autumn morning,
the moth resting on your finger.

Your dog, head bent,
collar jiggling, may tug
at his leash
to urge you home.

You may think of your coffee
growing cold
on the counter.
Sun in your eyes,
you may wish for a hat.

It is your task to sit still
and let the moth
shake its wet wings,
its tiny dark head.

You must invite the moth
to creep
on petite toothpick legs
to the nub of your bathrobe.

Your own breath quiet,
you must watch the moth
taxi up your belly,
across your chest.
Your heart may beat
a little faster,
the moth's earth's colored wings
rising.

# Lessons from the Chaparral

drink when you can,
doze in the sun,
feed birds,
blossom after rain

# Pact

My neighbor and her granddaughter
with faces broad as cauliflowers say,
"Just care for the cats and plants.
We stopped feeding that pesky dog.
Animal control will pick him up."
Their van, plump as a grape, glides off.
I tell my husband we could keep the dog.
He studies me. Illness has carved hollows

in my cheeks. I'm all long fingers and knees.
"You're not well enough. We can't interfere
with his owner's plans." Carrying cat food,
I hike up the hill. The dog that used to rush
at me, all paws and moving tail—a glad,
subservient streak of black ears and russet chest—
now stands still. Ribs poke through his fur.
When I brush past him, he wriggles his nose,

then turns as if he didn't smell biscuits in my pocket.
I slip inside my neighbor's house, dish Fancy Feast
in cats' bowls. Outside, I whistle and drop kibbles
like Gretel's bread crumbs in the dark grove
behind the house. At first, the wolf-dog
swallows kibbles whole. Then,
like a restaurant critic, he chews slowly.

His censored, half-throated cry ends in a wail.
I rub his thin back, pat his ears. "Quiet.
We can't be heard." Wetting trees
every 20 feet, he follows me and stops
just sort of the clearing. Back in sunlight,
I stand on asphalt. As if weary
from exercise, I brush hair off my forehead,
and wave to my husband from the road.

# Buying Rain Barrels in a Drought

The weather prophets have shouted for months
that El Niño rains were imminent.
A Sampson with sweat-shiny skin loads
two barrels that thump like thunder
in the trunk of our sedan. Only a few believers—
a couple in an old yellow Honda Civic
with *Coexist* on its bumper,
a man in a Padres ball cap, all customers
on this 90-degree November afternoon.
Too many winters of tumbleweed spinning
past the speed limit, of buckwheat and sage
crumbled like old toast. Un-sold umbrellas,
plaid, hot pink, too bright like party goers
at dawn, sit folded in corners of Rite Aid.
*Have faith,* the prophets of old said.
Believe what you can't see:
a town in the next valley,
a Japanese fisherman in a boat,
under stars
on the other side of your morning.

# Absent Friends

# Her Mail Unopened on the Table

I carry coffee to her cactus garden.
Honeysuckles, coral yuccas in bloom.
It is 100 in shade this Phoenix day.
Her little windmill and mesquite branches
hardly moving.

She must have bought these blue
mugs since my last visit.
I drove in the dark last night,
too late to say goodbye.

The wind picks up. Yuccas
and orange honeysuckles wave
and bend. The San Tan Mountains
disappear in the sudden pinwheel
of white.

I think of the rendezvous
of iceberg and ship and how
in old movies one scene
was wiped away,
replaced by another.
At noon, Dave and his son
from Phoenix Home Health
come to collect the bed, wheelchair,
and empty oxygen canisters.

# After His TV Dinner

not her good rice and chicken enchiladas,
his old demons are heating up
like heroin in a spoon.

In the nightly rustle of bed sheets,
her *What's the matter, honey?*
grows softer with each moonrise.

He hears her still, in each opening
of the bedroom door, every billowing
of her kitchen curtains.

Her long blue-black hair,
shiny as mussels at low tide.
Her smooth almond-scented skin.

These Phoenix mornings, he brews coffee
for one. Outside by her fountain,
purple lantanas bloom.

He watches sparrows peck
grass seed he planted,
this tender war with no truce.

# Requiem for Johnny

Once, a ball cap shading your eyes,
you were the ballet dancer,

Nureyev at second base,
leaping to catch the ball

in mid-flight.

Oh your blue, blue eyes
burning now.

Each night
we hand-washed

your scratchy uniform
for the next day's game.

Your throwing arm
ashes, flakes and bone.

Lips that kissed me.
Lips burning now, burning then,

when we were young.

# Minnow from Steve

*in memory of Steve Kowit*

My feet wiggle in wet sand. All the poets are singing:
Swinburne, Wordsworth, Keats, Shelley, and Steve
in his Brooklyn accent. I button my jacket, all wool,
10 bucks from Grants decades ago.
All the beaches I loved: my home town, Santa Monica,

with its apron of sand, Manhattan Beach with John
in our little red house on Valley Drive, now here
in Ocean Beach tracking the wise-cracking Jewish poet,
checked shirt and famous Levis, the ones that split,
reminding him of his mortality.

I search for his footsteps, those solid, wide imprints,
plump, deeper than mine. I walk where he walked
from Dog Beach to Cape May the street where
my daughter lives. When I was little, I read Longfellow:
*Often I think of that beautiful town that is seated by the sea.*
The sea has always been a poem, the poem
has always been a sea.

*She sang beyond the genius of the sea,* Stevens wrote.
He could have meant Steve. The message in the bottle
Steve wrote: save the minnow, save all the joyful fishes.

He could have meant all the poets he loved.
Po Chu I's white cranes are here, their yellow feet
planted in the rocks, the tide pools at Sunset Cliffs
where Steve once scooped the minnow and gave it back
to the sea. By a necklace of kelp, amber jewels

with white barnacle pearls, my feet slide inside
Steve's footprints. The waves wash over us. At last:
pelicans rising, pipers following.

# I'm in the Same White Shirt

with the tea stain at the hem
I wore when I saw you last.
Remember when you threatened
to bronze my old, beat up garden
shoes? You preserved wood ashes,
hollyhock seeds, remembered talks
from 7th grade. I'm forgetting
the exact ratio of green to yellow
in your eyes.

"How Carol of you," your mother,
daughters and I said when you held
on until the first day of spring.
Already today, I saw three
small towhees on the hibiscus.
And the lilacs opening.
Impossible not to feel a little glad.
How flagrant, promiscuous
and wild we were with your ashes.

Britlyn carried you on her surfboard,
spread bone flakes over kelp beds.
Your mother and Stephanie preserve
you in their roses. In ripped garden
shoes that would make you howl,
I water my share of you
with the purple Statice you bought
for me at Merrihew's Nursery
30 years ago.

# Each Morning I Sip Green Tea

# The Appointment

Liquid amber leaves, red, yellow
and gold skip across the patio
outside her office. I don't tell
my doctor this is the first time
out of my house since the last
time I saw her, how this time
I drove myself, how my hands
shook, the car veering off to
the edge of the road. How
I noticed the change of season
this late September. How my eyes
became an eager telescope, zoomed
in on a sunburst of blooming
fennel and a few green whiskers
on brown hills.

# 5 a.m.

I sip the sour, curdling potion
that is supposed to make
me well.
The morning star: a moony
white in a charcoal sky.
I stand at the kitchen sink,
considering. If I stay awake,
I could watch the sun rise
over our Rainbow Peak.
Our neighbor's rooster will
greet the yellow sky
with gusto. But then all day
I will be dragging myself
in my bathrobe from task
to task, the bathrobe cord
too tight at my waist. I rinse
the cup, glad the next dose
won't be for hours.
I wake again at noon.
Out the window, a moon-
colored piece of confetti
flies. Not confetti: first
butterfly of the season.

# Bats at Twilight

I ease myself into cool water,
bathing cap squeezing my ears.
First, I sink my feet and legs
in the cold. My baggy grandmother-
bathing suit's skirt balloons,
a mushroom-shaped bubble,
slaps my chest. The sun dying
past the junipers and cypress trees.
Water so cold I think of the ball-
player, Ted Williams, frozen now,
waiting to return to life.
I have to work to get well.
Holding onto the pink foam pool noodle,
I kick legs that shake when I stand,
yet still move slowly through water.
Bats fly out of the Brazilian
pepper tree, a whole cloud of them,
so close together, they look like
a black shroud. They can't see
my bathing cap. They hear
and aim for my chugging arms.

# Po Chu-I, Me, and a Thousand Fears

He worried
wind would blow his thatch roof away,
each apricot blossom would be his last,
each mountain visit, a farewell.

I worry
wind will blow my roof away,
my teeth will fall like apricot blossoms,
I will be a sack of stones
on my children's backs.

I slam the oven door
on these mosquito pies of worries,
waltz my coffee into the morning,
recite the rosary

of my children's names,
remember the comfort Po Chu-I found
in the view of Mt Lu
from his thatched hall,
the home he loved.

See the view I have now
from my California ranch house:
bees stagger like a certain Chinese poet
over fields of flowers,

snow peaked mountains,
orioles, pines, bamboo, myrtle
with purple blossoms.

## Two Venuses

My daughter hunts for perfect shoes
the day before her best friend's wedding.
Clicking steps, hair flying, she runs to
Famous Footwear, Marshall's, Ross,
Payless. My socks slide down into
my Mary Janes. I straggle, sag behind,
gulp thin March air. Afternoon sun slants
down on her red hair. A homesick breeze
flows west to the sea. Her quick steps,
the shape of her head, hair flapping
against her back, her swinging polka dot skirt,
her indented waist. A miniature Venus.
From the back, she looks like my mother.
She is the age my mother was when I was 2.
Suddenly I'm crawling over the setting sun,
the edge of afternoon. I stumble to my feet,
take slow baby-chick steps. Now
there are two Venuses to follow.
I always thought, if they had met,
they would have loved each other.
My mother, the ex-New Yorker,
sets a racing pace to Macy's. She tells
my daughter she saw a pair
of gold heels there just the other day.
Purses swinging on horseshoe hips,
alto laughs erupting in their throats,
arms linked, they will round the corner
and leave me behind. They pause
at Cinnabon. Two Venuses in synch,
they turn their heads, smile and wave
for me to catch up. I follow the scent
of sugar cookies.

# My Mother the Pantheist

said God was in the Anna hummingbird
and in the geranium Anna visited.
Anna's rose-pink throat to geraniums'
red petals. Anna's emerald feathers
to geraniums' open-handed green
leaves. God, she said, was in the spike
of blue columbine and in the man
with scuffed shoes selling newspapers
in front of Safeway. God, she said,
was in her and in me. When she died,
I had long talks with the dust-colored
spider weaving its web in the corner
of our kitchen. I whispered to the rocks
I pocketed from her garden.

# Each Week
## My Husband Buys Our Groceries

*after The Sick Wife, by Jane Kenyon*

He says he doesn't mind extra work.
Elegant in his Italian shoes, woven
cotton-shirt with epaulets,
he unloads the car. Cloth and paper
shopping bags brim with almond
milk, potatoes, carrots, leafy
green celery. Sometimes I stand
in the kitchen, in my bathrobe,
watch him fill silver bowls
with apples, line up our Italian
spices. Sometimes, I stay in our
bedroom. Sometimes, waking
from a nap, I hear the clink
and clang of tomato paste cans,
a love song.

# Each Morning I Sip Green Tea

luxuriate in honey scented
steam. Some mornings
I chant the names of my
absent friends, counting
backwards from the most
recent death: Susie, Kathleen
Joyce, John, Elbia, Joanne,
Carol, Susan.

They remind me this day
is mine. How lucky I am
to know new granddaughters,
friends still here, the unfolding
of daisies from another continent
here for me.
How lucky I am. Tea
from China, tea grown
in the valley of snow-covered
Mt. Lu, daises from what
once was Apartheid South
Africa. Shiny orange yellow
and pale pink flowers
we call freeway daisies.
How rich this world is.
How rich I am. Today
a yellow-throated warbler
lands on my white plastic
chair and sings to the palms,
to rabbits in the grass,
to the rich and the poor,
to the living and dead.

# Acknowledgments

All poems in this collection first appeared in these publications:

*By Line*
*California Quarterly*
*Cherry Blossom Review*
*Compass Rose*
*Earth's Daughters*
*Excuse Me I'm Writing*
*Hummingbird Review*
*In The Family*
*Knot Literary Journal*
*LIPS*
*Lucidity*
*Magee Park Poets*
*Our Reader's Quarterly*
*Paterson Literary Review*
*Paths: Notes from the Spiritual Journey*
*Persimmon*
*Phoebe*
*Poetry International*
*San Diego Arts & Culture*
*San Diego Poetry Annual*
*Sweet Annie & Sweet Pea*
*Synthesis*
*The Bridge*
*The Poetry Conspiracy*
*Writer's Resist*

# Credits

Cover art: *Woman with Newspaper Shoes*

photograph by TAAX

Cover Design: RILEY PRATO

Author photos: RAE ROSE

# Gratitude

Thank you:
 to MARIA MAZZIOTI GILLAN for her honest writing, her inspirational workshops, and big-hearted support;

 to MARGE PIERCY for her own "brilliant career" as an example of an independent spirit, and for her generosity;

 to the wonderful STEVE KOWIT, who mentored me as he had mentored so many others;

 to DIANE WAKOSKI, a pioneer in weaving the intimate with a personal mythology, for helping me find my way to what I hope is my own "inevitable garden," and for mentions in her *Lady of Light* (Anhinga Press: 2018);

 to the late LAURA BOSS, who pushed her own poetry and mine to new territory;

 to my poetry daughter LISA RATNIVARA, my spark plug;

 to the *Pleasures of Poetry* workshop over the past 18 years: founder and its leader HARRY GRISWOLD, fellow poets TERRY SPOHN, LENNY LIANE, R.T. SEDGWICK, TRISH DUGGER, DUKE SKAFF, MARTE BROEHM, and DICK EIDEN.

 to WENDY KLEIN for bringing family memories and her own poetic skills to my work;

 to my group of fearless women poets for continuous inspiration: KATHY O'FALLON, JONI GERSTEIN, CARRIE WEINBERGER, and AMANDA MATTIMOE;

 to SUZANNE O'CONNELL, for sharing her view of our home town, Santa Monica;

 to MATTHEW HEBERT, for generosity and a love of gardening that keeps me hopeful of new blossoms;

 to my granddaughters and grandsons, for inspiring joy;

 to JONATHAN FISHMAN, BARBARA GOMOLSKI, and SUSAN PRICE for teaching me to look for lessons in the chaparral;

 to RAE ROSE, D.H.R. FISHMAN, and most of all, to WILLIAM HARRY HARDING, for encouraging me to make this collection a reality.

# About the Poet

One of the first woman admitted to the American Film Institute in its screenwriting program, **Penny Perry** is an eight-time Pushcart Prize nominee in both Fiction and Poetry.

Her poetry has appeared in ***Lilith, Earth's Daughters, Lips, the Paterson Literary Review,*** and the ***San Diego Poetry Annual***, her fiction in ***Redbook*** and ***California Quarterly***.

Her first collection of poetry, **Santa Monica Disposal & Salvage,** appeared in 2012 (Garden Oak Press).

Perry's first novel, ***Selling Pencils, and Charlie*** (Lymer & Hart: 2021), was a finalist for the *San Diego Book Award*.

Her screenplay, ***A Berkeley Christmas***, first aired on PBS in 1973.

Her literary reviews have appeared in ***Poetry International*, Paterson Literary Review**, and online in *Excuse Me, I'm Writing.*

(excusemeimwriting.com)

She serves as a Fiction Editor for *Knot Literary Magazine*.

(knotliteraturemagazine.com)

Made in the USA
Columbia, SC
20 November 2024